GUIDE

MARSEILLE
RESTAURANT GUIDE

RESTAURANTS, BARS AND CAFES
Your Guide to Authentic Regional Eats

GUIDE BOOK FOR TOURIST

MARSEILLE RESTAURANT GUIDE 2022
Best Rated Restaurants in Marseille, France

© Victor K. Dumas
© E.G.P. Editorial

Printed in USA.

ISBN-13: 9798502688963

MARSEILLE RESTAURANT GUIDE

The Most Recommended Restaurants in Marseille

This directory is dedicated to the Business Owners and Managers who provide the experience that the locals and tourists enjoy. Thanks you very much for all that you do and thank for being the "People Choice".

Thanks to everyone that posts their reviews online and the amazing reviews sites that make our life easier.

The places listed in this book are the most positively reviewed and recommended by locals and travelers from around the world.

Thank you for your time and enjoy the directory that is designed with locals and tourist in mind!

TOP 500
RESTAURANTS
Ranked from #1 to #500

#1
Ummagumma
Cuisines: French, Tapas/Small Plates
Average price: Expensive
Area: Notre Dame du Mont
Address: 26 rue des Trois Rois
13006 Marseille France
Phone: 06 30 37 32 37

#2
Le Cercle Rouge
Cuisines: Tapas Bar, Corsican,
Cocktail Bar
Average price: Modest
Area: Thier
Address: 41 rue Adolphe Thiers
13001 Marseille France
Phone: 04 91 63 00 53

#3
Sauveur
Cuisines: Pizza, Italian
Average price: Modest
Area: Noailles
Address: 10 rue d'Aubagne
13001 Marseille France
Phone: 04 91 54 33 96

#4
Treize en Vue
Cuisines: Bistro, French
Average price: Modest
Area: Palais de Justice
Address: 40 rue de Breteuil
13006 Marseille France
Phone: 04 91 48 21 28

#5
Le Corto
Cuisines: Tapas/Small Plates, French,
Mediterranean
Average price: Modest
Area: Notre Dame du Mont
Address: 24 place Notre-Dame du Mont
13006 Marseille France
Phone: 04 91 53 19 50

#6
Le Café de la Banque
Cuisines: Brasserie, Bar
Average price: Modest
Area: Préfecture
Address: 24 bd Paul Peytral
13006 Marseille France
Phone: 04 91 33 35 07

#7
El Paséo
Cuisines: Spanish, Tapas/Small Plates
Average price: Modest
Area: Notre Dame du Mont
Address: 15 rue André Poggioli
13006 Marseille France
Phone: 04 96 12 03 30

#8
La Baie du Dragon
Cuisines: Chinese, Asian Fusion
Average price: Modest
Area: Notre Dame du Mont
Address: 8 place Notre Dame du Mont
13006 Marseille France
Phone: 04 91 92 74 78

#9
Bistro du Cours
Cuisines: French, Bistro
Average price: Expensive
Area: Notre Dame du Mont
Address: 13 Cours Julien
13006 Marseille France
Phone: 04 86 97 59 11

#10
O'Bidul
Cuisines: French
Average price: Modest
Area: Préfecture
Address: 79 rue de la Palud
13006 Marseille France
Phone: 04 91 33 93 78

#11
Le Duke
Cuisines: Bistro
Average price: Inexpensive
Area: Saint Victor
Address: 59 rue d'Endoume
13007 Marseille France
Phone: 04 91 90 74 21

#12
Le Grain de Sable
Cuisines: Vegetarian, French
Average price: Modest
Area: Belsunce
Address: 34 rue Baignoir
13001 Marseille France
Phone: 04 91 90 39 51

#13
L'Escapade Marseillaise
Cuisines: Mediterranean
Average price: Expensive
Area: Vauban
Address: 134 rue Paradis
13006 Marseille France
Phone: 04 91 31 61 69

#14
La Garbure
Cuisines: French Southwest
Average price: Expensive
Area: Notre Dame du Mont
Address: 9 cours Julien
13006 Marseille France
Phone: 04 91 47 18 01

#15
Vinonéo
Cuisines: French, Wine Bar, Mediterranean
Average price: Modest
Area: Hotel de Ville
Address: 6 place Daviel
13002 Marseille France
Phone: 04 91 90 40 26

#16
La Caravelle
Cuisines: French, Cafe, Wine Bar
Average price: Modest
Area: Hotel de Ville
Address: 34 quai du Port
13002 Marseille France
Phone: 04 91 90 36 64

#17
Aux Demoiselles du Mont
Cuisines: French
Average price: Modest
Area: Notre Dame du Mont
Address: 18 place Notre Dame du Mont
13006 Marseille France
Phone: 04 91 47 68 37

#18
La Cantine de Nour d'Egypte
Cuisines: Egyptian
Average price: Modest
Area: Saint Charles
Address: 10 rue Bernex
13001 Marseille France
Phone: 09 80 63 06 56

#19
Wadina
Cuisines: Lebanese, Halal, Vegetarian
Average price: Modest
Area: Vauban
Address: 133 rue Breteuil
13006 Marseille France
Phone: 04 91 48 28 91

#20
Chez Nous
Cuisines: French
Average price: Modest
Area: Notre Dame du Mont
Address: 22 place Notre Dame du Mont
13006 Marseille France
Phone: 04 91 37 66 24

#21
Le Marengo
Cuisines: Bar, Burgers, Brasserie
Average price: Modest
Area: Notre Dame du Mont
Address: 1 rue Marengo
13006 Marseille France
Phone: 09 64 47 32 40

#22
Mylan's Café
Cuisines: French, Cafe
Average price: Modest
Area: Vauban
Address: 146 rue Paradis
13006 Marseille France
Phone: 04 91 58 70 05

#23
Wasabi
Cuisines: Japanese
Average price: Modest
Area: Castellane
Address: 26 rue du Rouet
13006 Marseille France
Phone: 04 91 40 18 71

#24
Le Bouchon
Cuisines: French
Average price: Modest
Area: Castellane, Préfecture
Address: 26 rue Edmond Rostand
13006 Marseille France
Phone: 04 91 67 50 54

#25
L'Oléas
Cuisines: Mediterranean, French
Average price: Expensive
Area: Notre Dame du Mont
Address: 27 cours Julien
13006 Marseille France
Phone: 04 91 47 83 73

#26
Tako-San
Cuisines: Japanese
Average price: Modest
Area: Les Grandes Carmes
Address: 36 rue du Petit Puits
13002 Marseille France
Phone: 06 17 62 00 19

#27
Le Grain de Sel
Cuisines: French
Average price: Modest
Area: Opéra
Address: 39 rue de la Paix-Marcel-Paul
13001 Marseille France
Phone: 04 91 54 47 30

#28
Café Thaï
Cuisines: French, Thai,
Food Delivery Service
Average price: Modest
Area: Le Rouet
Address: 136 rue Rouet
13008 Marseille France
Phone: 04 91 25 44 45

#29
L'Arôme
Cuisines: Mediterranean
Average price: Expensive
Area: Notre Dame du Mont
Address: 9 rue des Trois Rois
13006 Marseille France
Phone: 04 91 42 88 80

#30
La Marche à Suivre
Cuisines: French, Steakhouse
Average price: Expensive
Area: Notre Dame du Mont
Address: 12 rue Vian
13006 Marseille France
Phone: 04 91 48 16 44

#31
Les Echevins
Cuisines: French, Mediterranean
Average price: Modest
Area: Opéra
Address: 44 rue Sainte
13001 Marseille France
Phone: 04 96 11 03 11

#33
L'Aromat'
Cuisines: Mediterranean, French
Average price: Expensive
Area: Opéra
Address: 49 rue Sainte
13001 Marseille France
Phone: 04 91 55 09 06

#32
Le Resto Provençal
Cuisines: Provencal
Average price: Modest
Area: Notre Dame du Mont
Address: 64 cours Julien
13006 Marseille France
Phone: 04 91 48 85 12

#34
Blonde et Brune
Cuisines: Tapas Bar, French, Mediterranean
Average price: Modest
Area: Palais de Justice
Address: 81 rue Breteuil
13006 Marseille France
Phone: 04 91 42 94 41

#35
Café Vian
Cuisines: Wine Bar, Provencal, Barbeque
Average price: Expensive
Area: Notre Dame du Mont
Address: 12 rue Vian
13006 Marseille France
Phone: 06 64 15 41 34

#36
Le Tian
Cuisines: French
Average price: Modest
Area: Les Cinq Avenues
Address: 47 bd de la Blancarde
13004 Marseille France
Phone: 04 91 25 81 45

#37
Zenji Café
Cuisines: Asian Fusion, Japanese
Average price: Inexpensive
Area: Les Cinq Avenues
Address: 24 rue Granoux
13004 Marseille France
Phone: 04 91 34 91 23

#38
Boudiou
Cuisines: Delis, Vegetarian, Salad
Average price: Modest
Area: Préfecture
Address: 13 bd Salvator
13006 Marseille France
Phone: 04 91 33 94 01

#39
La Tasca
Cuisines: Tapas Bar, Spanish
Average price: Modest
Area: La Conception
Address: 102 rue Ferrari
13005 Marseille France
Phone: 04 91 42 26 02

#40
Le Quinze
Cuisines: French
Average price: Modest
Area: Notre Dame du Mont
Address: 15 rue des Trois Rois
13006 Marseille France
Phone: 04 91 92 81 81

#41
La Cantine
Cuisines: Mediterranean
Average price: Expensive
Area: Opéra
Address: 27 cours Honoré d'Estienne d'Orves
13001 Marseille France
Phone: 04 91 33 37 08

#42
La Table Cinq
Cuisines: French
Average price: Expensive
Area: Les Cinq Avenues
Address: 13 bd de la Blancarde
13004 Marseille France
Phone: 04 91 34 85 22

#43
Coté Sud
Cuisines: French, Italian
Average price: Modest
Area: Les Cinq Avenues
Address: 28 rue Maréchal Fayolle
13004 Marseille France
Phone: 04 91 85 80 80

#44
Al Dente
Cuisines: Italian
Average price: Expensive
Area: Préfecture
Address: 10 rue Edmond Rostand
13006 Marseille France
Phone: 04 91 81 67 45

#45
Le Petit Flore
Cuisines: Brasserie
Average price: Modest
Area: Opéra
Address: 14 rue Corneille
13001 Marseille France
Phone: 04 91 33 86 53

#46
La Côte de Boeuf
Cuisines: French, Mediterranean
Average price: Expensive
Area: Opéra
Address: 35 cours Honoré d'Estienne d'Orves
13001 Marseille France
Phone: 04 91 33 00 25

#47
Axis
Cuisines: European,
Mediterranean, French
Average price: Expensive
Area: Castellane
Address: 8 rue de la Sainte Victoire
13006 Marseille France
Phone: 04 91 57 14 70

#48
L'Epuisette
Cuisines: French, Mediterranean
Average price: Exclusive
Area: Endoume
Address: 156 rue Vallon des Auffes
13007 Marseille France
Phone: 04 91 52 17 82

#49
Sur le Pouce
Cuisines: Mediterranean, Oriental, Halal
Average price: Inexpensive
Area: Belsunce
Address: 2 rue des Convalescents
13001 Marseille France
Phone: 04 91 56 13 28

#50
Le Patio du Prado
Cuisines: French
Average price: Modest
Area: Le Rouet
Address: 9 rue Borde
13008 Marseille France
Phone: 04 91 40 61 43

#51
Le Terroir Corse
Cuisines: Corsican
Average price: Modest
Area: Notre Dame du Mont
Address: 20 place Notre Dame du Mont
13006 Marseille France
Phone: 04 96 12 07 26

#52
Le Carré Bistromanie
Cuisines: Brasserie
Average price: Exclusive
Area: Le Pharo
Address: 36 bd Charles Livon
13007 Marseille France
Phone: 04 91 15 59 60

#53
La Vieille Pelle
Cuisines: Italian
Average price: Modest
Area: Hotel de Ville
Address: 37 ave de Saint Jean
13002 Marseille France
Phone: 04 91 90 62 00

#54
Le Pavillon Thaï
Cuisines: Thai, Vietnamese, Asian Fusion
Average price: Modest
Area: Notre Dame du Mont
Address: 28 rue des 3 Frères Barthélemy
13006 Marseille France
Phone: 04 96 12 46 19

#55
L'Eléphant Rose à Pois Blancs
Cuisines: Ice Cream & Frozen Yogurt,
Creperies, Desserts
Average price: Inexpensive
Area: Notre Dame du Mont
Address: 3 rue des Trois Rois
13006 Marseille France
Phone: 04 91 47 34 68

#56
Chez Simone
Cuisines: French
Average price: Modest
Area: Thier
Address: 23 cours Franklin Roosevelt
13001 Marseille France
Phone: 09 54 51 38 87

#57
César Place
Cuisines: European, French, Farmers
Market, Mediterranean
Average price: Modest
Area: Opéra
Address: 21 place aux Huiles
13001 Marseille France
Phone: 04 91 33 25 22

#58
L'Ambassade de Bretagne
Cuisines: Creperies, Breakfast & Brunch
Average price: Modest
Area: Opéra
Address: 43 rue Sainte
13001 Marseille France
Phone: 04 91 01 41 29

#59
Nam Viet
Cuisines: Cafe
Average price: Inexpensive
Area: Opéra
Address: 23 place Huiles
13001 Marseille France
Phone: 04 91 33 36 58

#60
La Cantinetta
Cuisines: Italian
Average price: Expensive
Area: Notre Dame du Mont
Address: 24 cours Julien
13006 Marseille France
Phone: 04 91 48 10 48

#61
La Traversée du Grec
Cuisines: Greek
Average price: Modest
Area: Notre Dame du Mont
Address: 17 rue des Trois Rois
13006 Marseille France
Phone: 04 91 48 07 30

#62
Relais Corse
Cuisines: Corsican, Wine Bar
Average price: Modest
Area: Castellane
Address: 49 avenue du Prado
13006 Marseille France
Phone: 09 50 72 99 53

#63
Urban Kitchen
Cuisines: French, Bar, Breakfast & Brunch
Average price: Modest
Area: Lodi
Address: 23 ave de Corinthe
13006 Marseille France
Phone: 09 83 72 01 66

#64
Biiig
Cuisines: Burgers, Asian Fusion, Vietnamese
Average price: Modest
Area: Castellane
Address: 8 rue Louis Maurel
13006 Marseille France
Phone: 04 91 37 00 11

#65
Le Boucher
Cuisines: Steakhouse, European
Average price: Expensive
Area: Castellane
Address: 10 rue de Village
13006 Marseille France
Phone: 04 91 48 79 65

#66
La Marmarita
Cuisines: Middle Eastern
Average price: Modest
Area: Notre Dame du Mont, Le Camas
Address: 6 rue St Pierre
13006 Marseille France
Phone: 04 91 47 07 03

#67
Le Petit Nice - Passedat
Cuisines: French, Seafood
Average price: Exclusive
Area: Endoume
Address: 17 rue des Braves
13007 Marseille France
Phone: 04 91 59 25 92

#68
Le Bistrot à Vin
Cuisines: Bistro, Wine Bar, Mediterranean
Average price: Modest
Area: Opéra
Address: 17 rue Sainte
13001 Marseille France
Phone: 04 91 54 02 20

#69
29 Place aux Huiles
Cuisines: French
Average price: Expensive
Area: Opéra
Address: 29 place aux Huiles
13001 Marseille France
Phone: 04 91 33 26 44

#70
Videodrome 2
Cuisines: Cinema, Cafe
Average price: Inexpensive
Area: Notre Dame du Mont
Address: 49 cours Julien
13006 Marseille France
Phone: 04 91 42 75 41

#71
Le Jardin des Arts
Cuisines: French
Average price: Expensive
Area: Les Cinq Avenues
Address: 53 rue Marx Dormoy
13004 Marseille France
Phone: 04 91 24 92 38

#72
La Maison des Raviolis
Cuisines: Dim Sum, Asian Fusion
Average price: Modest
Area: Préfecture
Address: 14 rue d'Italie
13006 Marseille France
Phone: 04 91 94 59 98

#73
Minakouk
Cuisines: Mediterranean, Tea Room
Average price: Modest
Area: Notre Dame du Mont
Address: 21 rue Fontange
13006 Marseille France
Phone: 04 91 53 54 55

#74
La Passarelle
Cuisines: French, Mediterranean
Average price: Expensive
Area: Saint Victor
Address: 52 rue Plan Fourmiguier
13007 Marseille France
Phone: 04 91 33 03 27

#75
Limone
Cuisines: Italian
Average price: Modest
Area: Palais de Justice
Address: 32 boulevard Notre-Dame
13006 Marseille France
Phone: 04 91 91 47 64

#76
Le Julien
Cuisines: Lyonnais, Mediterranean,
French Southwest
Average price: Expensive
Area: Palais de Justice
Address: 114 rue Paradis
13006 Marseille France
Phone: 04 91 37 06 22

#77
Déjeuner en Ville
Cuisines: Bistro
Average price: Modest
Area: Hotel de Ville
Address: 5 rue de la République
13002 Marseille France
Phone: 04 91 90 35 59

#78
La Table de l'Olivier
Cuisines: European
Average price: Expensive
Area: La Joliette
Address: 56 rue Mazenod
13002 Marseille France
Phone: 04 91 91 17 04

#79
Le Débouché
Cuisines: Wine Bar, French
Average price: Modest
Area: Les Réformés
Address: 3 bd National
13001 Marseille France
Phone: 04 91 50 96 25

#80
Friterie Werner & Co
Cuisines: Belgian, Fast Food
Average price: Inexpensive
Area: Thier
Address: 9 rue Guy Môquet
13001 Marseille France
Phone: 06 89 90 58 14

#81
Eden Roc
Cuisines: Corsican, Mediterranean
Average price: Modest
Area: Le Pharo
Address: 52 corniche John Kennedy
13007 Marseille France
Phone: 04 91 31 06 66

#82
La Grand Baie
Cuisines: Cajun/Creole, Indian
Average price: Expensive
Area: Lodi
Address: 28 cours Gouffé
13006 Marseille France
Phone: 04 91 80 33 77

#83
La Source de Jade
Cuisines: Asian Fusion, Vietnamese
Average price: Modest
Area: Notre Dame du Mont
Address: 3 rue Trois Frères Barthélémy
13006 Marseille France
Phone: 04 91 48 87 09

#84
La Folle Epoque
Cuisines: Brasserie
Average price: Modest
Area: Préfecture
Address: 10 place Félix Baret
13006 Marseille France
Phone: 04 91 33 38 24

#85
Toinou
Cuisines: Seafood, Seafood Market
Average price: Expensive
Area: Noailles
Address: 3 cours Saint-Louis
13001 Marseille France
Phone: 04 91 33 14 94

#86
El Santo Cachon
Cuisines: Latin American
Average price: Modest
Area: La Conception
Address: 40 rue Ferrari
13005 Marseille France
Phone: 06 95 99 45 93

#87
Bar des 13 Coins
Cuisines: Bar, Cafe, Mediterranean
Average price: Modest
Area: La Joliette
Address: 45 rue Sainte-Françoise
13002 Marseille France
Phone: 04 91 91 56 49

#88
Moon Burger
Cuisines: Fast Food, Burgers
Average price: Inexpensive
Area: Saint Victor
Address: 29 bd de la Corderie
13007 Marseille France
Phone: 04 91 01 74 86

#89
Le 12 Mermoz
Cuisines: French, American
Average price: Inexpensive
Area: Périer
Address: 12 rue Jean Mermoz
13008 Marseille France
Phone: 04 91 57 02 27

#90
Chez Les Garçons
Cuisines: Corsican
Average price: Expensive
Area: Préfecture
Address: 8 rue Lafon
13006 Marseille France
Phone: 04 91 33 14 46

#91
Ko-Ishi
Cuisines: Japanese, Creperies, Sushi Bar
Average price: Modest
Area: Opéra
Address: 25 rue Sainte
13001 Marseille France
Phone: 04 91 04 64 10

#92
Casa No Name
Cuisines: French, Mediterranean
Average price: Expensive
Area: Notre Dame du Mont
Address: 7 rue André Poggioli
13006 Marseille France
Phone: 04 91 47 75 82

#93
Taste
Cuisines: Sandwiches, Salad, Fast Food
Average price: Modest
Area: La Joliette
Address: 51 rue de Forbin
13002 Marseille France
Phone: 06 28 04 91 38

#94
Une Table au Sud
Cuisines: Mediterranean
Average price: Exclusive
Area: Hotel de Ville
Address: 2 quai du Port
13002 Marseille France
Phone: 04 91 90 63 53

#95
Le Mas
Cuisines: French
Average price: Expensive
Area: Opéra
Address: 4 rue Lulli
13001 Marseille France
Phone: 04 91 33 25 90

#96
La Virgule
Cuisines: French
Average price: Expensive
Area: Hotel de Ville
Address: 27 rue de la Loge
13002 Marseille France
Phone: 04 91 90 91 11

#97
Les Buvards
Cuisines: Beer, Wine & Spirits,
French, Wine Bar
Average price: Modest
Area: Hotel de Ville
Address: 34 grand rue
13002 Marseille France
Phone: 04 91 90 69 98

#98
La Part des Anges
Cuisines: Bistro, Tapas Bar,
Beer, Wine & Spirits
Average price: Modest
Area: Opéra
Address: 33 rue Sainte
13001 Marseille France
Phone: 04 91 33 55 70

#99
La Velada
Cuisines: Mediterranean, Pizza
Average price: Expensive
Area: Saint Victor
Address: 31 rue Endoume
13007 Marseille France
Phone: 04 91 52 93 68

#100
Kim-Do
Cuisines: Japanese
Average price: Expensive
Area: Les Cinq Avenues
Address: 4 rue Capazza
13004 Marseille France
Phone: 04 91 34 00 08

#101
Delouss
Cuisines: Italian
Average price: Inexpensive
Area: Préfecture
Address: 5 rue Dieudé
13006 Marseille France
Phone: 04 91 91 65 14

#102
L'Authentique
Cuisines: Fast Food, Sandwiches, Creperies
Average price: Inexpensive
Area: Castellane
Address: 9 place Castellane
13006 Marseille France
Phone: 04 91 53 91 79

#103
Le Goût des Choses
Cuisines: French
Average price: Expensive
Area: Notre Dame du Mont
Address: 4 place Notre-Dame du Mont
13006 Marseille France
Phone: 04 91 48 70 62

#104
Le Péron
Cuisines: European, Seafood
Average price: Exclusive
Area: Endoume
Address: 56 Corniche Kennedy
13007 Marseille France
Phone: 04 91 52 15 22

#105
La Cuisine Republique of Marseille
Cuisines: French
Average price: Modest
Area: Hotel de Ville
Address: 5 rue Coutellerie
13002 Marseille France
Phone: 04 91 31 92 49

#106
Le Phénicia
Cuisines: Middle Eastern
Average price: Modest
Area: Saint Charles
Address: 187 bd de la Libération
13001 Marseille France
Phone: 04 91 50 43 77

#107
Paule & Kopa
Cuisines: Mediterranean
Average price: Expensive
Area: Opéra
Address: 42 place aux Huiles
13001 Marseille France
Phone: 04 91 33 26 03

#108
Le Vésuvio
Cuisines: Italian, Pizza
Average price: Modest
Area: Saint Lambert
Address: 33 rue Decazes
13007 Marseille France
Phone: 04 91 52 44 27

#109
Le Caribou
Cuisines: Corsican
Average price: Expensive
Area: Opéra
Address: 38 place Thiars
13001 Marseille France
Phone: 06 74 90 57 64

#110
Trattoria Marco
Cuisines: Italian, Brasserie
Average price: Modest
Area: Hotel de Ville
Address: 2 rue de la Guirlande
13002 Marseille France
Phone: 04 91 90 60 08

#111
P.P.MAULIO
Cuisines: Pizza, Corsican
Average price: Modest
Area: Opéra
Address: 24 rue Sainte
13001 Marseille France
Phone: 04 91 33 46 13

#112
La Raclette
Cuisines: Fondue, French
Average price: Modest
Area: Notre Dame du Mont
Address: 23 cours Julien
13006 Marseille France
Phone: 04 91 47 19 69

#113
Lauracée
Cuisines: French
Average price: Expensive
Area: Opéra
Address: 96 rue Grignan
13001 Marseille France
Phone: 04 91 33 63 36

#114
L'Alimentation Générale
Cuisines: Tapas/Small Plates, Bar,
Mediterranean
Average price: Modest
Area: Saint Victor
Address: 34 rue du Plan Fourmiguier
13007 Marseille France
Phone: 04 91 33 04 68

#115
Bobolivo
Cuisines: Brasserie, Bistro, French
Average price: Modest
Area: Hotel de Ville
Address: 29 rue Caisserie
13002 Marseille France
Phone: 04 91 31 38 21

#116
Les Arcenaulx
Cuisines: French, Bookstore
Average price: Expensive
Area: Opéra
Address: 25 cours Estiennes d'Orves
13001 Marseille France
Phone: 04 91 59 80 30

#117
Le Fémina
Cuisines: Arabian
Average price: Expensive
Area: Noailles
Address: 1 rue du Musée
13001 Marseille France
Phone: 04 91 54 03 56

#118
Le Zinc
Cuisines: French, Mediterranean
Average price: Expensive
Area: Le Rouet
Address: 182 rue du Rouet
13008 Marseille France
Phone: 04 91 78 23 44

#119
Le Baron Perché
Cuisines: Italian, French, Mediterranean
Average price: Modest
Area: Saint Lambert
Address: 45 rue Châteaubriand
13007 Marseille France
Phone: 09 51 24 89 52

#120
Au Bout du Quai
Cuisines: French, Mediterranean
Average price: Expensive
Area: Hotel de Ville
Address: 1 avenue St Jean
13002 Marseille France
Phone: 04 91 99 53 36

#121
Les Panisses
Cuisines: French, Brasserie
Average price: Modest
Area: Opéra
Address: 23 rue Sainte
13001 Marseille France
Phone: 04 91 52 86 83

#122
Le Chalet du Pharo
Cuisines: Mediterranean, French
Average price: Expensive
Area: Le Pharo
Address: 58 bd Charles Livon
13007 Marseille France
Phone: 04 91 52 80 11

#123
Victor Café
Cuisines: Mediterranean, Lounge,
Breakfast & Brunch
Average price: Expensive
Area: Le Pharo
Address: 71 bd Charles Livon
13007 Marseille France
Phone: 04 88 00 46 00

#124
Le Citronnier
Cuisines: French, International, South African
Average price: Modest
Area: La Blancarde
Address: 2 rue Elemir Bourges
13004 Marseille France
Phone: 04 91 85 48 18

#125
Ghomrassen
Cuisines: Moroccan
Average price: Inexpensive
Area: Belsunce
Address: 21 bd Dugommier
13001 Marseille France
Phone: 04 86 77 17 49

#126
La Tarraillette
Cuisines: French, Lyonnais, Wine Bar
Average price: Exclusive
Area: Le Camas
Address: 59 bd Eugène Pierre
13005 Marseille France
Phone: 04 91 48 91 48

#127
Le Jardin d'à Côté
Cuisines: Mediterranean
Average price: Modest
Area: Notre Dame du Mont
Address: 65 Cours Julien
13006 Marseille France
Phone: 04 91 94 15 51

#128
Bistrot l'Horloge
Cuisines: Bistro, French, Wine Bar
Average price: Modest
Area: Opéra
Address: 11 A cours Honoré d'Estienne
d'Orves, 13001 Marseille France
Phone: 09 50 41 39 66

#129
La Cantine du Midi
Cuisines: Vegetarian
Average price: Inexpensive
Area: La Belle de Mai
Address: 36 rue Bernard
13003 Marseille France
Phone: 07 60 78 04 52

#130
Chez Vincent - Il Vesuvio
Cuisines: Pizza, Italian, Mediterranean
Average price: Modest
Area: Opéra
Address: 25 rue Glandevès
13001 Marseille France
Phone: 04 91 33 96 78

#131
Restaurant La Villa
Cuisines: French
Average price: Expensive
Area: Saint Giniez
Address: 113 ave Jean Mermoz
13008 Marseille France
Phone: 04 91 71 21 11

#132
Le Relais 50
Cuisines: Mediterranean, French, Gastropub
Average price: Expensive
Area: Hotel de Ville
Address: 18 quai du Port
13002 Marseille France
Phone: 04 91 52 52 50

#133
La Maronaise Café
Cuisines: Cafe, Brasserie
Average price: Expensive
Area: La Plage
Address: 2 place de l'Amiral Muselier
13008 Marseille France
Phone: 04 91 76 63 93

#134
Vapiano
Cuisines: Italian
Average price: Modest
Area: Castellane
Address: 20 ave du Prado
13006 Marseille France
Phone: 04 91 48 83 35

#135
Vaggy
Cuisines: Cafe, Breakfast & Brunch, Bar
Average price: Modest
Area: Lodi
Address: 87 rue de Lodi
13006 Marseille France
Phone: 04 88 64 31 12

#136
L'Entrecôte du Port
Cuisines: Steakhouse, French
Average price: Modest
Area: Opéra
Address: 6 quai de Rive Neuve
13001 Marseille France
Phone: 04 91 33 84 84

#137
La Table à Deniz
Cuisines: French, Mediterranean
Average price: Modest
Area: Opéra
Address: 63 rue Sainte
13007 Marseille France
Phone: 04 91 54 19 74

#138
Les Quatre Epices
Cuisines: French
Average price: Modest
Area: Les Cinq Avenues
Address: 30 Boulevard Georges Clemenceau
13004 Marseille France
Phone: 04 91 49 47 99

#139
Le Fantastique
Cuisines: French, Wine Bar, Bistro
Average price: Modest
Area: Lodi
Address: 76 bd Baille
13006 Marseille France
Phone: 09 73 52 99 46

#140
Malthazar
Cuisines: French, Bistro, Brasserie
Average price: Expensive
Area: Opéra
Address: 19 rue Fortia
13001 Marseille France
Phone: 04 91 33 42 46

#141
Longchamp Palace
Cuisines: Brasserie, Bistro,
Breakfast & Brunch
Average price: Modest
Area: Les Réformés
Address: 22 bd Longchamp
13001 Marseille France
Phone: 04 91 50 76 13

#142
La Jonque Viet
Cuisines: Chinese
Average price: Modest
Area: Les Cinq Avenues
Address: 28 rue Maréchal Fayolle
13004 Marseille France
Phone: 04 91 49 70 38

#143
Bar de la Mairie
Cuisines: Cafe
Average price: Modest
Area: Hotel de Ville
Address: 66 Quai du Port
13002 Marseille France
Phone: 04 91 90 06 33

#144
Rouge Belle de Mai
Cuisines: French, Jazz & Blues
Average price: Modest
Area: La Belle de Mai
Address: 47 rue Fortuné Jourdan
13003 Marseille France
Phone: 04 91 07 00 87

#145
La Table Ronde
Cuisines: Creperies, French
Average price: Expensive
Area: Préfecture
Address: 24 rue Sylvabelle
13006 Marseille France
Phone: 04 91 04 68 83

#146
La Folie du Burger
Cuisines: Burgers, Fast Food
Average price: Modest
Area: Lodi
Address: 5 ave de Toulon
13006 Marseille France
Phone: 09 81 36 68 36

#147
What's Up?
Cuisines: French, Tapas Bar, Burgers
Average price: Modest
Area: Thier
Address: 98 rue Curiol
13001 Marseille France
Phone: 09 83 67 72 07

#148
On Dine
Cuisines: French
Average price: Expensive
Area: Hotel de Ville
Address: 22 rue de la Guirlande
13002 Marseille France
Phone: 09 83 53 83 41

#149
Chez Didier et Brigitte
Cuisines: Pizza
Average price: Modest
Area: Lodi
Address: 97 rue de Tilsit
13006 Marseille France
Phone: 04 91 47 37 57

#150
Chez Étienne
Cuisines: Pizza, Italian
Average price: Modest
Area: Les Grandes Carmes
Address: 43 rue de Lorette
13002 Marseille France
Phone: 04 91 54 76 33

#151
L'Eau à la Bouche
Cuisines: Pizza
Average price: Modest
Area: Endoume
Address: 120 corniche du Président Kennedy
13007 Marseille France
Phone: 04 91 52 16 16

#152
L'Entre Pots
Cuisines: French, Wine Bar
Average price: Modest
Area: Les Réformés
Address: 22 cours Joseph Thierry
13001 Marseille France
Phone: 09 50 78 40 05

#153
La Table de Casimir
Cuisines: Italian
Average price: Modest
Area: Préfecture
Address: 21 rue d'Italie
13006 Marseille France
Phone: 04 91 81 95 18

#154
La Fabrique
Cuisines: Tapas/Small Plates, French
Average price: Expensive
Area: Hotel de Ville
Address: 3 place jules verne
13002 Marseille France
Phone: 04 91 91 40 48

#155
Le Comptoir Dugommier
Cuisines: Brasserie
Average price: Modest
Area: Les Réformés
Address: 14 bd Dugommier
13001 Marseille France
Phone: 09 50 12 32 62

#156
Le Gran Café
Cuisines: Bistro, Mediterranean
Average price: Modest
Area: Saint Giniez
Address: 158 rue Jean Mermoz
13008 Marseille France
Phone: 04 91 22 70 84

#157
Rowing Club de Marseille
Cuisines: French
Average price: Expensive
Area: Le Pharo
Address: 34 boulevard Charles Livon
13007 Marseille France
Phone: 04 91 90 07 78

#158
Le Bocal
Cuisines: French
Average price: Modest
Area: Hotel de Ville
Address: 58 quai du Port
13002 Marseille France
Phone: 06 60 73 13 13

#159
La Piazza Papa
Cuisines: Italian, Pizza, Salad
Average price: Modest
Area: Saint Victor
Address: 15 quai Rive Neuve
13007 Marseille France
Phone: 04 91 59 82 24

#160
Chez Fonfon
Cuisines: Seafood
Average price: Exclusive
Area: Endoume
Address: 140 rue Vallon des Auffes
13007 Marseille France
Phone: 04 91 52 14 38

#161
Bar Marengo
Cuisines: Cafe, Cocktail Bar
Average price: Inexpensive
Area: Opéra
Address: 21 rue Saint Saëns
13001 Marseille France
Phone: 04 91 33 18 61

#162
Le Bistrot des Dames
Cuisines: Bistro
Average price: Expensive
Area: Opéra
Address: 34 place aux Huiles
13001 Marseille France
Phone: 06 99 22 25 03

#163
WAAW
Cuisines: Party & Event Planning, Bistro
Average price: Modest
Area: Notre Dame du Mont
Address: 17 rue Pastoret
13006 Marseille France
Phone: 04 91 42 16 33

#164
Les 3 Léo O' Chalet du Jardin
Cuisines: French, Tea Room
Average price: Modest
Area: Saint Victor
Address: 2 A rue Vauvenargues
13007 Marseille France
Phone: 04 91 31 06 59

#165
L'Estaminet Matinal
Cuisines: French, Cafe
Average price: Inexpensive
Area: Notre Dame du Mont
Address: 12 place Notre-Dame-du-Mont
13006 Marseille France
Phone: 04 91 92 93 15

#166
QI Restaurant
Cuisines: Asian Fusion, Mediterranean
Average price: Modest
Area: Palais de Justice
Address: 72 rue de la Paix Marcel Paul
13006 Marseille France
Phone: 04 86 97 26 77

#167
Pouce
Cuisines: Tea Room, Mediterranean
Average price: Modest
Area: Saint Charles
Address: 95 bd Longchamp
13001 Marseille France
Phone: 09 52 73 32 21

#168
Café de l'Abbaye
Cuisines: Bistro, Cafe, Brasserie
Average price: Modest
Area: Saint Victor
Address: 3 Rue d'Endoume
13007 Marseille France
Phone: 04 91 33 44 67

#169
Bar Bû
Cuisines: Fish & Chips, Burgers, Cocktail Bar
Average price: Modest
Area: Opéra
Address: 8 rue Euthymenes
13001 Marseille France
Phone: 04 88 64 44 37

#170
Bar le Trash
Cuisines: Cafe, Bar
Average price: Inexpensive
Area: Baille
Address: 28 Rue Berceau
13005 Marseille France
Phone: 04 91 25 52 16

#171
Lan Thaï
Cuisines: Thai
Average price: Modest
Area: Notre Dame du Mont
Address: 13 rue Vian
13006 Marseille France
Phone: 04 91 37 22 30

#172
Au Vieux Clocher
Cuisines: Pizza, French
Average price: Modest
Area: Hotel de Ville
Address: 12 place des Augustines
13002 Marseille France
Phone: 04 91 90 84 39

#173
Le Quai du Rire
Cuisines: Comedy Club, Cafe
Average price: Modest
Area: Saint Victor
Address: 16 quai Rive Neuve
13007 Marseille France
Phone: 04 91 54 95 00

#174
Il caffé
Cuisines: Bistro, Cafe, Coffee & Tea
Average price: Modest
Area: Notre Dame du Mont
Address: 63 Cours Julien
13006 Marseille France
Phone: 04 91 42 02 19

#175
Arigato Sushi
Cuisines: Sushi Bar
Average price: Modest
Area: Noailles
Address: 16 bd Garibaldi
13001 Marseille France
Phone: 04 91 33 13 13

#176
Le Champ de Mars
Cuisines: Bar, Cafe
Average price: Inexpensive
Area: Notre Dame du Mont
Address: 12 rue André Poggioli
13006 Marseille France
Phone: 04 91 42 51 87

#177
Burger and Coffee
Cuisines: Burgers, Bagels
Average price: Modest
Area: Thier
Address: 11 rue Théâtre Français
13001 Marseille France
Phone: 09 51 45 54 61

#178
Café Bovo
Cuisines: European
Average price: Modest
Area: Opéra
Address: 9 rue Beauvau
13001 Marseille France
Phone: 04 91 31 56 99

#179
Cyprien
Cuisines: French
Average price: Exclusive
Area: Lodi
Address: 56 avenue Toulon
13006 Marseille France
Phone: 04 91 25 50 00

#180
Le Café des Épices
Cuisines: French, Mediterranean
Average price: Expensive
Area: Hotel de Ville
Address: 4 rue du Lacydon
13002 Marseille France
Phone: 04 91 91 22 69

#181
Le Bistro Vénitien
Cuisines: Pizza, French, Thai
Average price: Modest
Area: Notre Dame du Mont
Address: 29 cours Julien
13006 Marseille France
Phone: 04 91 47 34 34

#182
Sushi Resto
Cuisines: Sushi Bar, Japanese
Average price: Modest
Area: Préfecture
Address: 27 bis rue d'Italie
13006 Marseille France
Phone: 04 91 47 13 03

#183
L'Effet Clochette
Cuisines: French
Average price: Modest
Area: Hotel de Ville
Address: 2 place des Augustines
13001 Marseille France
Phone: 06 20 93 00 24

#184
Piment Thaï
Cuisines: Thai
Average price: Modest
Area: Notre Dame du Mont
Address: 4 cours Lieutaud
13001 Marseille France
Phone: 04 91 31 17 01

#185
A l'Ile de la Réunion
Cuisines: Cajun/Creole
Average price: Modest
Area: Opéra
Address: 14 rue de la Paix
13001 Marseille France
Phone: 04 91 31 94 43

#186
Le Comptoir Marseillais
Cuisines: Bar, Tapas Bar, Mediterranean
Average price: Expensive
Area: La Plage
Address: 5 Promenade Georges Pompidou
13008 Marseille France
Phone: 04 91 32 92 54

#187
Thaï Baie
Cuisines: Thai
Average price: Expensive
Area: Opéra
Address: 6 rue Corneille
13001 Marseille France
Phone: 04 91 54 15 23

#188
La Morada
Cuisines: Mexican
Average price: Modest
Area: Notre Dame du Mont
Address: 5 rue Crudère
13006 Marseille France
Phone: 06 48 13 43 57

#189
La Palangrotte
Cuisines: French
Average price: Expensive
Area: Notre Dame du Mont
Address: 13 rue Crudere
13006 Marseille France
Phone: 04 91 47 54 26

#190
Chez Madie - Les Galinettes
Cuisines: Mediterranean
Average price: Expensive
Area: Hotel de Ville
Address: 138 Quai du Port
13002 Marseille France
Phone: 04 91 90 40 87

#191
Le Bistrot Asiatique
Cuisines: Asian Fusion
Average price: Modest
Area: Palais de Justice
Address: 54 rue Breteuil
13006 Marseille France
Phone: 04 91 98 17 68

#192
O'Brady's Irish Pub
Cuisines: Pub, Brasserie, Irish Pub
Average price: Modest
Area: Sainte Anne
Address: 378 avenue de Mazargues
13008 Marseille France
Phone: 04 91 71 53 71

#193
Chez Mama Africa
Cuisines: African
Average price: Modest
Area: Noailles
Address: 57 rue d'Aubagne
13001 Marseille France
Phone: 04 91 33 75 33

#194
Le Moulin de la Galette
Cuisines: Creperies
Average price: Modest
Area: Les Cinq Avenues
Address: 35 Ave Maréchal Foch
13004 Marseille France
Phone: 04 91 34 80 65

#195
La Trilogie des Cepages
Cuisines: French
Average price: Exclusive
Area: Opéra
Address: 35 rue Paix Marcel Paul
13001 Marseille France
Phone: 04 91 33 96 03

#196
La Cour du Palais
Cuisines: French
Average price: Expensive
Area: Opéra
Address: 24 rue Fortia
13001 Marseille France
Phone: 04 91 54 34 07

#197
Le Capriccio
Cuisines: Pizza, Italian
Average price: Modest
Area: Saint Charles
Address: 70 bd Camille Flammarion
13001 Marseille France
Phone: 06 27 03 41 99

#198
Abaco
Cuisines: French
Average price: Modest
Area: Le Pharo
Address: 38 rue Papety
13007 Marseille France
Phone: 04 91 90 23 73

#199
Le Petit Pavillon
Cuisines: French, Beaches, Lounge
Average price: Modest
Area: Endoume
Address: 54 Corniche du Président John
Fitzgerald Kennedy
13007 Marseille France
Phone: 04 91 31 00 38

#200
Bar de la Marine
Cuisines: Brasserie, Bar, Cafe
Average price: Modest
Area: Saint Victor
Address: 15 quai de Rive Neuve
13001 Marseille France
Phone: 04 91 54 95 42

#201
Namasté
Cuisines: Indian
Average price: Modest
Area: Castellane
Address: 43 ave du Prado
13006 Marseille France
Phone: 04 91 80 57 94

#202
Dos Hermanas
Cuisines: Tapas/Small Plates, Spanish
Average price: Modest
Area: Notre Dame du Mont
Address: 18 rue Bussy l'Indien
13006 Marseille France
Phone: 04 96 12 00 23

#203
Côté Rue
Cuisines: French
Average price: Modest
Area: Hotel de Ville
Address: 14 rue saint Pons
13002 Marseille France
Phone: 04 91 90 66 36

#204
Tien-Tsin Cotier
Cuisines: Chinese
Average price: Modest
Area: Hotel de Ville
Address: 3 place jules verne
13002 Marseille France
Phone: 04 91 90 47 96

#205
Café T'Ine
Cuisines: Cafe, Coffee & Tea, Salad
Average price: Modest
Area: Hotel de Ville
Address: 17 rue Caisserie
13002 Marseille France
Phone: 06 63 20 78 50

#206
Restaurant Midi Pile
Cuisines: Cafe
Average price: Modest
Area: Palais de Justice
Address: 63 rue Breteuil
13006 Marseille France
Phone: 04 91 81 44 28

#207
Adonis du Liban
Cuisines: Lebanese
Average price: Modest
Area: Notre Dame du Mont
Address: 10-12 rue des Trois Rois
13006 Marseille France
Phone: 04 91 48 00 14

#208
Le Mélo
Cuisines: Dance Club, Karaoke, American
Average price: Modest
Area: Notre Dame du Mont
Address: 68 cours Julien
13006 Marseille France
Phone: 04 91 42 77 68

#209
Au Coeur du Panier
Cuisines: French
Average price: Expensive
Area: Les Grandes Carmes
Address: 18 rue du Panier
13002 Marseille France
Phone: 04 91 91 65 80

#210
Jaipur
Cuisines: Indian
Average price: Modest
Area: Opéra
Address: 2 quai de Rive Neuve
13001 Marseille France
Phone: 04 91 33 07 03

#211
Kyo Sushi
Cuisines: Japanese, Sushi Bar
Average price: Modest
Area: Castellane
Address: 15 ave du Prado
13006 Marseille France
Phone: 04 84 25 15 11

#212
Le Majestic
Cuisines: Chinese
Average price: Modest
Area: La Conception
Address: 211 Rue St Pierre
13005 Marseille France
Phone: 04 91 48 30 37

#213
Mama Shelter Restaurant
Cuisines: French, Mediterranean
Average price: Expensive
Area: Notre Dame du Mont
Address: 64 rue de la Loubière
13006 Marseille France
Phone: 04 84 35 21 00

#214
Viens Attendre
Cuisines: Cafe
Average price: Modest
Area: Saint Charles
Address: Quai A
13001 Marseille France
Phone: 06 99 33 20 21

#215
Chez Gilda
Cuisines: Food Stand
Average price: Inexpensive
Area: Thier
Address: 13 rue des Trois Mages
13006 Marseille France
Phone: 06 62 17 90 46

#216
Green Bear Coffee
Cuisines: Cafe, Gluten-Free, Vegetarian
Average price: Modest
Area: Préfecture
Address: 22 bd Paul Peytral
13006 Marseille France
Phone: 09 50 38 88 29

#217
Massena Café
Cuisines: Cafe
Average price: Modest
Area: Castellane
Address: 1 avenue Jules Cantini
13006 Marseille France
Phone: 04 91 78 18 10

#218
Le Perroquet Bleu
Cuisines: Brasserie, Tapas/Small Plates
Average price: Modest
Area: La Joliette
Address: 72 bd des Dames
13002 Marseille France
Phone: 04 95 09 65 13

#219
Nul Part Ailleurs
Cuisines: Provencal
Average price: Modest
Area: Saint Victor
Address: 18 quai Rive Neuve
13001 Marseille France
Phone: 04 91 33 58 95

#220
Les Trois Rois
Cuisines: French
Average price: Exclusive
Area: Notre Dame du Mont
Address: 24 Rue Des 3 rois
13006 Marseille France
Phone: 04 91 53 44 84

#221
Café-Restaurant les Grandes Tables
Cuisines: Wine Bar, French, Cafe
Average price: Modest
Area: La Belle de Mai
Address: 41 rue Jobin
13003 Marseille France
Phone: 04 95 04 95 85

#222
Bistrot Haxo
Cuisines: French, Breakfast & Brunch, Cafe
Average price: Modest
Area: Opéra
Address: 6 rue Haxo
13001 Marseille France
Phone: 04 91 33 42 71

#223
Cafouch aux Saveurs
Cuisines: Cafe
Average price: Modest
Area: La Joliette
Address: 20 rue Mazenod
13002 Marseille France
Phone: 04 91 31 67 14

#224
Restaurant Il Canaletto
Cuisines: Cafe
Average price: Modest
Area: Opéra
Address: 6 Cours Jean Ballard
13001 Marseille France
Phone: 04 91 33 90 12

#225
Schilling
Cuisines: French, Seafood
Average price: Modest
Area: Hotel de Ville
Address: 37 rue Caisserie
13002 Marseille France
Phone: 04 91 01 81 39

#226
Le Caveau du Théâtre
Cuisines: Mediterranean, French
Average price: Modest
Area: Hotel de Ville
Address: 19 Place Lenche
13002 Marseille France
Phone: 04 91 91 58 84

#227
Douceur Piquante
Cuisines: French, African
Average price: Modest
Area: Hotel de Ville
Address: 17 rue de l'Eveché
13002 Marseille France
Phone: 06 35 21 73 69

#228
Café Populaire
Cuisines: Mediterranean, Cafe
Average price: Expensive
Area: Palais de Justice
Address: 110 rue Paradis
13006 Marseille France
Phone: 04 91 02 53 96

#229
Le Panier Gourmand
Cuisines: Mediterranean, Cafe
Average price: Modest
Area: Hotel de Ville
Address: 5 rue Four du Chapitre
13002 Marseille France
Phone: 04 91 90 95 11

#230
Pizza Le Saint Jean
Cuisines: Pizza
Average price: Inexpensive
Area: Hotel de Ville
Address: 54 Bis avenue St Jean
13002 Marseille France
Phone: 04 91 91 41 88

#231
Le Terminus
Cuisines: French, Brasserie, Cafe
Average price: Modest
Area: Saint Barnabé
Address: 2 place du Caire
13012 Marseille France
Phone: 04 91 49 41 60

#232
Chez Michel
Cuisines: French
Average price: Exclusive
Area: Le Pharo
Address: 6 rue des Catalans
13007 Marseille France
Phone: 04 91 52 30 63

#233
El Picoteo
Cuisines: Spanish, Tapas/Small Plates
Average price: Modest
Area: La Conception
Address: 53 rue Saint Pierre
13005 Marseille France
Phone: 09 83 51 09 98

#234
La Coupole Provencale
Cuisines: French, Brasserie
Average price: Modest
Area: Opéra
Address: 5 rue Haxo
13001 Marseille France
Phone: 04 91 54 88 57

#235
Le Cours-en-Vert
Cuisines: Cafe, Vegetarian
Average price: Modest
Area: Notre Dame du Mont
Address: 102 cours Julien
13006 Marseille France
Phone: 06 75 06 97 90

#236
Big Fernand
Cuisines: Burgers
Average price: Modest
Area: La Joliette
Address: Les Docks
13002 Marseille France
Phone: 09 87 65 43 21

#237
Terra di Sicilia
Cuisines: Italian
Average price: Modest
Area: Castellane
Address: 34 rue du Docteur Jean Fiolle
13006 Marseille France
Phone: 09 50 13 58 28

#238
La Cave à Jambon
Cuisines: Spanish, Tapas/Small Plates
Average price: Modest
Area: Saint Victor
Address: 89 rue Sainte
13007 Marseille France
Phone: 09 67 46 75 79

#239
Set Squash
Cuisines: Sports Club, French
Average price: Expensive
Area: Sainte Anne
Address: 265 av de Mazargues
13008 Marseille France
Phone: 04 91 71 94 71

#240
Le Tatao
Cuisines: African
Average price: Modest
Area: Les Réformés
Address: 16 rue Grande Armée
13001 Marseille France
Phone: 04 91 62 66 45

#241
Apsara
Cuisines: Cambodian
Average price: Expensive
Area: Saint Victor
Address: 151 rue Sainte
13007 Marseille France
Phone: 04 91 55 55 71

#242
Salumeria Giuppo
Cuisines: Italian
Average price: Expensive
Area: Thier
Address: 7 bd de Libération
13001 Marseille France
Phone: 09 81 86 35 95

#243
Sahtein
Cuisines: Lebanese
Average price: Inexpensive
Area: Belsunce
Address: 2 rue Henri Fiocca
13001 Marseille France
Phone: 04 88 04 65 74

#244
U-percut
Cuisines: Music Venues,
Wine Bar, Tapas Bar
Average price: Modest
Area: Saint Victor
Address: 127 rue Sainte
13007 Marseille France
Phone: 06 60 96 78 88

#245
Le 20 260
Cuisines: Corsican
Average price: Expensive
Area: Opéra
Address: 44 rue Saint-Saëns
13001 Marseille France
Phone: 04 91 11 70 30

#246
L'Arbre à Pains
Cuisines: Sandwiches
Average price: Inexpensive
Area: Hotel de Ville
Address: 28 rue de la Bonneterie
13002 Marseille France
Phone: 06 83 29 34 35

#247
Kitch&Bio
Cuisines: Sandwiches, European, Desserts
Average price: Modest
Area: Opéra
Address: 30 rue Fortia
13001 Marseille France
Phone: 06 14 44 24 69

#248
Le Poulpe
Cuisines: French, Mediterranean,
Breakfast & Brunch
Average price: Expensive
Area: Hotel de Ville
Address: 84 quai du Port
13002 Marseille France
Phone: 04 95 09 15 91

#249
Greendeliss
Cuisines: Desserts, Salad, Soup
Average price: Inexpensive
Area: Les Cinq Avenues
Address: 11 avenue du Maréchal Foch
13004 Marseille France
Phone: 09 86 23 04 58

#250
Emilio
Cuisines: Italian, Convenience Stores
Average price: Expensive
Area: Saint Giniez
Address: 70 avenue de Mazargue
13008 Marseille France
Phone: 04 91 32 67 76

#251
La Kahena
Cuisines: French, Turkish, Mediterranean
Average price: Modest
Area: Belsunce
Address: 2 rue de la République
13001 Marseille France
Phone: 04 91 90 61 93

#252
Coeur d'Asie
Cuisines: Cafe
Average price: Modest
Area: Sainte Anne
Address: 38 boulevard Barral
13008 Marseille France
Phone: 04 91 22 73 60

#253
La Maison Michel
Cuisines: Bakeries, Sandwiches
Average price: Inexpensive
Area: Opéra
Address: 33 rue Vacon
13001 Marseille France
Phone: 04 91 33 79 43

#254
Le Cirque
Cuisines: Cafe
Average price: Exclusive
Area: Hotel de Ville
Address: 118 Quai Port
13002 Marseille France
Phone: 04 91 91 08 91

#255
Brasserie des Templiers
Cuisines: Bar, Cafe, Brasserie
Average price: Modest
Area: Belsunce
Address: 27 rue Reine Elisabeth
13001 Marseille France
Phone: 04 91 90 03 54

#256
Le Clan des Cigales
Cuisines: Arts & Crafts, Mediterranean
Average price: Modest
Area: Les Grandes Carmes
Address: 8 rue du Petit Puits
13002 Marseille France
Phone: 06 63 78 07 83

#257
La Parenthèse
Cuisines: Wine Bar, Tapas/Small Plates,
Mediterranean
Average price: Modest
Area: La Vieille Chapelle
Address: 2 impasse de Riou
13008 Marseille France
Phone: 06 83 05 62 05

#258
Le Massilia Café
Cuisines: Mediterranean, French Southwest
Average price: Inexpensive
Area: Belsunce
Address: 33 rue Reine Elisabeth
13001 Marseille France
Phone: 04 91 91 82 14

#259
Burger's Banquet
Cuisines: Burgers
Average price: Modest
Area: Opéra
Address: 9 rue Molière
13001 Marseille France
Phone: 04 91 93 32 40

#260
Le Vin Sobre
Cuisines: Wine & Spirits, Bistro, Brasserie
Average price: Modest
Area: Saint Giniez
Address: 56 Rue Négresko
13008 Marseille France
Phone: 04 91 32 68 64

#261
La Madone
Cuisines: Lounge, Italian, Mediterranean
Average price: Exclusive
Area: Hotel de Ville
Address: 92-94 Quai du Port
13002 Marseille France
Phone: 04 91 91 26 26

#262
Au Lamparo
Cuisines: Mediterranean
Average price: Modest
Area: Hotel de Ville
Address: 4 Place Lenche
13002 Marseille France
Phone: 04 91 90 90 29

#263
Shangai Express
Cuisines: Fast Food
Average price: Modest
Area: Saint Barnabé
Address: 19 ave de Saint Julien
13012 Marseille France
Phone: 04 91 34 67 99

#264
Le Cherche Midi
Cuisines: Fast Food, Salad
Average price: Modest
Area: Saint Giniez
Address: 33 bd Edouard Herriot
13008 Marseille France
Phone: 04 91 71 20 76

#265
Brasserie du Stade
Cuisines: Cafe
Average price: Modest
Area: Saint Giniez
Address: 26 boulevard Michelet
13008 Marseille France
Phone: 04 91 22 03 45

#266
Restaurant Pizzeria Chez Dédé
Cuisines: Pizza
Average price: Modest
Area: Le Camas
Address: 60 rue George
13005 Marseille France
Phone: 04 91 42 41 90

#267
Question de Goût
Cuisines: French
Average price: Modest
Area: La Vieille Chapelle
Address: 147 avenue Joseph Vidal
13008 Marseille France
Phone: 04 91 73 59 08

#268
Le Kashmir Lounge
Cuisines: Indian
Average price: Modest
Area: Opéra
Address: 18 rue de la Paix
13001 Marseille France
Phone: 04 91 54 99 72

#269
Carbone
Cuisines: French
Average price: Expensive
Area: Opéra
Address: 22 rue Sainte
13001 Marseille France
Phone: 04 91 55 52 73

#270
Staow Café
Cuisines: Bistro, Lounge
Average price: Inexpensive
Area: Le Pharo
Address: 10 rue des Catalans
13007 Marseille France
Phone: 04 96 17 54 15

#271
La Table d'Helios
Cuisines: Greek, Delicatessen, Caterer
Average price: Inexpensive
Area: Les Cinq Avenues
Address: 221 bd de la Libération
13004 Marseille France
Phone: 09 53 40 60 14

#272
Les Indécis
Cuisines: Bar, French
Average price: Modest
Area: Saint Victor
Address: 139 rue Sainte
13007 Marseille France
Phone: 04 95 09 66 47

#273
L'Anse du Panier
Cuisines: French, Bar
Average price: Modest
Area: La Joliette
Address: 16 rue Jean François Lecas
13002 Marseille France
Phone: 04 91 91 22 95

#274
Zia Concetta
Cuisines: Trattorie, Imported Food
Average price: Modest
Area: Saint Lambert
Address: 111 rue d'Endoume
13007 Marseille France
Phone: 06 36 82 12 52

#275
La Boîte à Sardine
Cuisines: Seafood Market, Seafood
Average price: Expensive
Area: Thier
Address: 2 bd de la Libération
13001 Marseille France
Phone: 04 91 50 95 95

#276
Riz D'or
Cuisines: Chinese
Average price: Modest
Area: Les Cinq Avenues
Address: 21 ave des Chartreux
13004 Marseille France
Phone: 04 91 08 88 94

#277
Le 8ème Sud
Cuisines: French
Average price: Modest
Area: La Plage
Address: 51 promenade Georges Pompidou
13008 Marseille France
Phone: 04 91 71 57 42

#278
O'Stop
Cuisines: Bistro, Brasserie, French
Average price: Modest
Area: Opéra
Address: 16 rue Saint-Saëns
13001 Marseille France
Phone: 04 91 33 85 34

#279
L'Ombre de Marx
Cuisines: Comic Books, French
Average price: Modest
Area: Notre Dame du Mont
Address: 20 rue des Trois Frères Barthélémy
13006 Marseille France
Phone: 04 91 48 71 32

#280
La Manne
Cuisines: French, Mediterranean
Average price: Modest
Area: Les Réformés
Address: 18 bd de la Liberté
13001 Marseille France
Phone: 04 91 08 77 39

#281
La Terrasse de Domino
Cuisines: Mediterranean
Average price: Exclusive
Area: Sainte Marguerite
Address: 1 bd Paul Claudel
13009 Marseille France
Phone: 04 91 41 92 78

#282
La Fiesta
Cuisines: Dance Club, Pub, Burgers
Average price: Modest
Area: Notre Dame du Mont
Address: 6a rue Crudère
13006 Marseille France
Phone: 04 91 48 26 17

#283
Il Primo
Cuisines: Italian
Average price: Modest
Area: Sainte Anne
Address: 7 avenue Alexandre Dumas
13008 Marseille France
Phone: 04 91 77 90 17

#284
Okaasan
Cuisines: Japanese
Average price: Expensive
Area: Notre Dame du Mont
Address: 9 rue des Trois Rois
13006 Marseille France
Phone: 06 65 75 56 22

#285
Dame Oseille
Cuisines: French, Brasserie
Average price: Modest
Area: Les Réformés
Address: 14 Cours Joseph Thierry
13001 Marseille France
Phone: 04 91 62 03 76

#286
Chez Jeannot
Cuisines: Pizza, Italian
Average price: Expensive
Area: Endoume
Address: 129 rue Vallon des Auffes
13007 Marseille France
Phone: 04 91 52 11 28

#287
Brasserie Paulaner
Cuisines: Brasserie, French
Average price: Expensive
Area: Castellane
Address: 8 avenue Prado
13006 Marseille France
Phone: 04 91 37 95 96

#288
Tabi No Yume
Cuisines: Japanese
Average price: Modest
Area: Sainte Anne
Address: 1 bd Sainte-Anne
13008 Marseille France
Phone: 04 91 22 09 33

#289
Quelques Saveurs du Sud
Cuisines: Italian, Mediterranean
Average price: Modest
Area: Mazargues
Address: 37 bd Concorde
13009 Marseille France
Phone: 04 91 40 09 87

#290
Les Akolytes
Cuisines: French, European
Average price: Expensive
Area: Le Pharo
Address: 41 rue Papety
13007 Marseille France
Phone: 04 91 59 17 10

#291
L'Hippocampe
Cuisines: Seafood, Mediterranean
Average price: Modest
Area: Hotel de Ville
Address: 14 quai du Port
13002 Marseille France
Phone: 04 91 90 88 38

#292
Le Ventre de l'Architecte
Cuisines: French
Average price: Expensive
Area: Sainte Anne
Address: 280 bd Michelet
13008 Marseille France
Phone: 04 91 16 78 23

#293
Santa Pizza
Cuisines: Pizza
Average price: Modest
Area: Saint Victor
Address: 88 rue Sainte
13007 Marseille France
Phone: 04 91 54 44 34

#294
Le Grand Escalier
Cuisines: Brasserie
Average price: Modest
Area: Belsunce
Address: 39 boulevard d'Athènes
13001 Marseille France
Phone: 04 91 31 75 65

#295
La Table de l'Empereur
Cuisines: Vietnamese
Average price: Modest
Area: Sainte Marguerite
Address: 101 Boulevard Sainte-Marguerite
13009 Marseille France
Phone: 04 91 75 98 36

#296
Duc Dat
Cuisines: Asian Fusion
Average price: Modest
Area: Sainte Marguerite
Address: 320 bd Romain Rolland
13010 Marseille France
Phone: 04 91 75 61 65

#297
Le Vieux Moulin
Cuisines: French
Average price: Modest
Area: Les Cinq Avenues
Address: 12 rue de Provence
13004 Marseille France
Phone: 04 91 26 12 12

#298
Le Dernier Métro
Cuisines: Tobacco Shop, Brasserie
Average price: Modest
Area: Le Camas
Address: 68 bd Eugène Pierre
13005 Marseille France
Phone: 04 91 47 32 11

#299
L'Aromence
Cuisines: Brasserie, Provencal
Average price: Modest
Area: Le Rouet
Address: 8-12 rue Liandier
13008 Marseille France
Phone: 04 96 20 27 84

#300
Le Balagan
Cuisines: Soup, Desserts, Salad
Average price: Modest
Area: Le Rouet
Address: 99 rue Rouet
13008 Marseille France
Phone: 04 91 71 72 13

#301
Il Piccolo
Cuisines: Italian
Average price: Modest
Area: Baille
Address: 187 bd Baille
13005 Marseille France
Phone: 04 91 02 86 74

#302
Place Lorette
Cuisines: Moroccan, Concept Shop
Average price: Expensive
Area: Les Grandes Carmes
Address: 3 place de Lorette
13002 Marseille France
Phone: 09 81 35 66 75

#303
Le Cityzen
Cuisines: French, Cafe
Average price: Expensive
Area: Palais de Justice
Address: 3 rue Joseph Autran
13006 Marseille France
Phone: 04 30 22 03 29

#304
Le Pointu
Cuisines: Bar, Brasserie, Tapas Bar
Average price: Modest
Area: Opéra
Address: 18 cours Honoré d'Estienne d'Orves
13001 Marseille France
Phone: 04 91 55 61 53

#305
Avam
Cuisines: Tea Room, French, Salad
Average price: Inexpensive
Area: Saint Barnabé
Address: 18 rue du Docteur Cauvin
13012 Marseille France
Phone: 04 91 25 92 24

#306
Bar des Maraîchers
Cuisines: Pub, Cafe
Average price: Inexpensive
Area: Thier
Address: 100 rue Curiol
13001 Marseille France
Phone: 04 91 48 44 89

#307
La Terrasse du Panier
Cuisines: Mediterranean
Average price: Modest
Area: Les Grandes Carmes
Address: 10 place Pistoles
13002 Marseille France
Phone: 04 91 52 93 06

#308
Liban Express
Cuisines: Lebanese
Average price: Modest
Area: Les Chartreux
Address: 12 bd de roux
13004 Marseille France
Phone: 04 91 40 50 00

#309
Le Dome
Cuisines: Brasserie
Average price: Modest
Area: Lodi
Address: 71 bd Baille
13006 Marseille France
Phone: 04 91 58 83 17

#310
L'Ecomotive
Cuisines: Cafe, Shared Office Spaces
Average price: Modest
Area: Belsunce
Address: 2 place des Marseillaises
13001 Marseille France
Phone: 06 52 35 83 31

#311
Chez Vincent
Cuisines: Pizza
Average price: Modest
Area: Les Cinq Avenues
Address: 2 Bis ave Chartreux
13004 Marseille France
Phone: 04 91 49 62 34

#312
Axum
Cuisines: Ethiopian
Average price: Modest
Area: Préfecture
Address: 14 rue d'Italie
13006 Marseille France
Phone: 04 91 48 95 97

#313
OM Café
Cuisines: Brasserie, Sports Bar
Average price: Expensive
Area: Opéra
Address: 25 quai des Belges
13001 Marseille France
Phone: 04 91 33 80 33

#314
Yoj
Cuisines: Sushi Bar, Ramen
Average price: Modest
Area: Belsunce
Address: 17 cours Belsunce
13001 Marseille France
Phone: 04 91 89 69 59

#315
Kim Chi
Cuisines: Chinese, Vietnamese
Average price: Modest
Area: Saint Charles
Address: 91 boulevard Libération
13001 Marseille France
Phone: 04 91 50 98 44

#316
Nguyen Hoang
Cuisines: Asian Fusion
Average price: Modest
Area: Hotel de Ville
Address: 6 rue Mery
13002 Marseille France
Phone: 04 91 90 71 92

#317
Le Palais d'Asie
Cuisines: Cafe
Average price: Modest
Area: Sainte Anne
Address: 33 boulevard Luce
13008 Marseille France
Phone: 04 91 76 10 03

#318
Sushi Street Café
Cuisines: Sushi Bar, Japanese
Average price: Expensive
Area: Palais de Justice
Address: 24 bd Notre Dame
13006 Marseille France
Phone: 04 91 54 17 90

#319
Chez Noel
Cuisines: Pizza, Italian
Average price: Modest
Area: Les Réformés
Address: 174 la Canebière
13001 Marseille France
Phone: 04 91 42 17 22

#320
Le Petit Montmartre
Cuisines: Brasserie
Average price: Modest
Area: Notre Dame du Mont
Address: 17 place N D du Mont
13006 Marseille France
Phone: 04 91 92 61 72

#321
L'Eurasien
Cuisines: Asian Fusion
Average price: Modest
Area: Notre Dame du Mont
Address: 57 cours Julien
13006 Marseille France
Phone: 04 91 48 56 16

#322
Elyssa
Cuisines: Arabian, Middle Eastern,
Mediterranean
Average price: Modest
Area: Saint Victor
Address: 26 quai de Rive Neuve
13007 Marseille France
Phone: 04 91 56 00 81

#323
La Piazza
Cuisines: Italian
Average price: Expensive
Area: Castellane
Address: 12 place Castellane
13006 Marseille France
Phone: 04 91 57 10 57

#324
Pizza Charly
Cuisines: Pizza
Average price: Inexpensive
Area: Noailles
Address: 24 rue des Feuillants
13001 Marseille France
Phone: 09 84 20 79 62

#325
Le Taxi Brousse
Cuisines: Dance Club, African
Average price: Modest
Area: Les Grandes Carmes
Address: 21 rue Observance
13002 Marseille France
Phone: 04 91 56 26 57

#326
Le David
Cuisines: Brasserie
Average price: Expensive
Area: La Plage
Address: 101 promenade Georges-Pompidou
13008 Marseille France
Phone: 04 91 79 99 63

#327
Chez Lê
Cuisines: Vietnamese
Average price: Inexpensive
Area: Baille
Address: 96 rue Roger Brun
13005 Marseille France
Phone: 04 91 25 78 38

#328
Da Romano
Cuisines: Italian
Average price: Modest
Area: Castellane
Address: 229 rue Paradis
13006 Marseille France
Phone: 04 91 48 53 66

#329
La Table du Chef
Cuisines: French, European
Average price: Expensive
Area: Le Cabot
Address: 83 bd du Redon
13009 Marseille France
Phone: 04 91 75 04 55

#330
L'Horloge du Cap Est
Cuisines: French, Breakfast & Brunch, Cafe
Average price: Modest
Area: Saint Loup
Address: 7 impasse Ferdinand Arnodin
13010 Marseille France
Phone: 04 91 79 22 72

#331
L'Egoïste
Cuisines: Bistro, French
Average price: Modest
Area: Opéra
Address: 28 cours Honore d'Estiennes d'Orves
13001 Marseille France
Phone: 06 95 61 45 92

#332
Le Môle Passedat - La Table
Cuisines: French
Average price: Expensive
Area: La Joliette
Address: 1 Esplanade du J4
13002 Marseille France
Phone: 04 91 19 17 81

#333
Latté
Cuisines: French, Pub, Tapas Bar
Average price: Modest
Area: Hotel de Ville
Address: 16 rue de l'Évêché
13002 Marseille France
Phone: 06 65 30 35 36

#334
La Chope d'Or
Cuisines: Cafe
Average price: Modest
Area: Hotel de Ville
Address: 32 Quai Port
13002 Marseille France
Phone: 04 91 91 10 72

#335
Le Chaperon Rouge
Cuisines: French
Average price: Modest
Area: Palais de Justice
Address: 16 Cours Pierre Puget
13006 Marseille France
Phone: 04 91 33 79 25

#336
Georges
Cuisines: Brasserie
Average price: Modest
Area: Le Camas
Address: 115 bd Chave
13005 Marseille France
Phone: 09 84 30 53 28

#337
Soir d'Asie
Cuisines: Chinese, Vietnamese
Average price: Expensive
Area: La Joliette
Address: 121 Rue de l'Evêché
13002 Marseille France
Phone: 04 91 90 21 07

#338
Black Stone
Cuisines: Pub, Pizza, Brasserie
Average price: Modest
Area: Sainte Marguerite
Address: 10 bd Ganay
13009 Marseille France
Phone: 06 20 06 16 53

#339
La Pizzeria des Catalans
Cuisines: Mediterranean, Pizza
Average price: Exclusive
Area: Le Pharo
Address: 3 rue des Catalans
13007 Marseille France
Phone: 04 91 52 37 82

#340
El Kantaoui
Cuisines: Mediterranean, Tea Room
Average price: Modest
Area: Belsunce
Address: 53 rue Aix
13001 Marseille France
Phone: 04 91 91 05 94

#341
Restaurant des Chutes Lavie
Cuisines: French
Average price: Inexpensive
Area: Les Chutes Lavies
Address: 45 avenue des Chutes Lavie
13004 Marseille France
Phone: 04 91 64 28 62

#342
Pizza Chez Romain
Cuisines: Pizza, Food Truck
Average price: Modest
Area: Le Camas
Address: 13005 Marseille France
Phone: 06 09 52 82 21

#343
Restaurant Chez Loury
Cuisines: Seafood
Average price: Expensive
Area: Opéra
Address: 3 rue Fortia
13001 Marseille France
Phone: 04 91 33 09 73

#344
La Cocotte a des Plumes
Cuisines: Art Galleries, Tea Room, French
Average price: Modest
Area: Préfecture
Address: 79 rue de la Palud
13006 Marseille France
Phone: 04 91 33 93 78

#345
Oscar's Bagels and Sandwiches
Cuisines: Sandwiches, Bagels, French
Average price: Inexpensive
Area: Opéra
Address: 8 quai de Rive-Neuve
13001 Marseille France
Phone: 04 91 33 28 86

#346
A Casa
Cuisines: Italian, Cafe, Coffee & Tea
Average price: Modest
Area: Opéra
Address: 45 rue Sainte
13001 Marseille France
Phone: 04 91 33 68 74

#347
Les Danaïdes
Cuisines: Brasserie, Bar
Average price: Modest
Area: Les Réformés
Address: 4-6 square Stalingrad
13001 Marseille France
Phone: 04 91 62 28 51

#348
Pascal's Kitchen
Cuisines: Thai, French
Average price: Expensive
Area: La Pointe Rouge
Address: 46 ave de Montredon
13008 Marseille France
Phone: 04 91 06 35 53

#349
Les Trois Forts
Cuisines: Mediterranean, French
Average price: Exclusive
Area: Endoume
Address: 36 bd Charles Livon
13007 Marseille France
Phone: 04 91 15 59 56

#350
Il Gusto d'Oro
Cuisines: Pizza, Italian
Average price: Modest
Area: Préfecture
Address: 109 rue du Paradis
13006 Marseille France
Phone: 04 13 24 23 80

#351
Café de la Gare
Cuisines: Cafe
Average price: Modest
Area: Sainte Anne
Address: 201 avenue de Mazargues
13008 Marseille France
Phone: 06 23 08 41 06

#352
Bar le Trianon
Cuisines: French, Bar
Average price: Modest
Area: Opéra
Address: 32 rue Sainte
13001 Marseille France
Phone: 04 91 33 86 14

#353
Restaurant Côté Jardin
Cuisines: French
Average price: Expensive
Area: Baille
Address: 232 boulevard Baille
13005 Marseille France
Phone: 04 91 80 49 55

#354
MundArt
Cuisines: Venues & Event Spaces, Asian
Fusion, Art Galleries
Average price: Modest
Area: La Joliette
Address: 70-72 rue de la Joliette
13002 Marseille France
Phone: 04 91 45 44 90

#355
La Rocha
Cuisines: Lebanese
Average price: Modest
Area: La Plage
Address: 45 Pro Georges Pompidou
13008 Marseille France
Phone: 04 91 22 20 81

#356
Le Sunset
Cuisines: Brasserie, Bistro
Average price: Modest
Area: Bompard
Address: 315 corniche Kennedy
13007 Marseille France
Phone: 04 91 59 18 45

#357
Culti
Cuisines: Lounge, Mediterranean,
Tobacco Shop
Average price: Expensive
Area: Bompard
Address: 222 chemin Roucas Blanc
13007 Marseille France
Phone: 04 91 90 80 92

#358
Jeroboam
Cuisines: Brasserie
Average price: Expensive
Area: Le Rouet
Address: 100 avenue Jules Cantini
13006 Marseille France
Phone: 04 91 40 47 55

#359
L'Osteria du Prado
Cuisines: Italian, Pizza
Average price: Modest
Area: Castellane
Address: 84 ave du Prado
13006 Marseille France
Phone: 04 91 92 98 64

#360
Shanghai Kitchen
Cuisines: Shanghainese
Average price: Modest
Area: Opéra
Address: 14 cours Jean Ballard
13001 Marseille France
Phone: 09 54 68 60 62

#361
Le Kenji
Cuisines: Asian Fusion, Vietnamese
Average price: Modest
Area: Saint Julien
Address: 18 ave de la Figone
13012 Marseille France
Phone: 04 91 35 27 10

#362
Le Caucase
Cuisines: Lebanese
Average price: Modest
Area: Lodi
Address: 59 ave de Toulon
13006 Marseille France
Phone: 04 91 77 92 25

#363
Hoang
Cuisines: Chinese, Vietnamese, Asian Fusion
Average price: Inexpensive
Area: Saint Pierre
Address: 73 bd Jeanne d'Arc
13005 Marseille France
Phone: 04 91 47 14 06

#364
Bombay Grill
Cuisines: Indian, Pakistani
Average price: Inexpensive
Area: La Plage
Address: 79 Promenade Georges Pompidou
13008 Marseille France
Phone: 04 91 41 68 10

#365
Un Jardin en Ville
Cuisines: French
Average price: Modest
Area: Saint Giniez
Address: 22 ave de Mazargues
13008 Marseille France
Phone: 04 91 76 68 16

#366
Brocante Café
Cuisines: French, Breakfast & Brunch, Cafe
Average price: Modest
Area: Castellane, Vauban
Address: 146 rue Paradis
13006 Marseille France
Phone: 04 91 81 63 07

#367
Le Yen Seiiki
Cuisines: Japanese, Sushi Bar, Food
Delivery Service
Average price: Expensive
Area: Castellane
Address: 60 ave du Prado
13008 Marseille France
Phone: 04 91 53 00 09

#368
Au quai 68
Cuisines: Cafe, Sandwiches, Coffee & Tea
Average price: Modest
Area: Saint Pierre
Address: 336 bd Chave
13005 Marseille France
Phone: 09 81 90 17 77

#369
KIM BA
Cuisines: French
Average price: Modest
Area: Notre Dame du Mont
Address: 21 cours Julien
13006 Marseille France
Phone: 04 91 42 81 59

#370
Kortchma
Cuisines: Russian, Ukrainian
Average price: Expensive
Area: Notre Dame du Mont
Address: 30 rue des Trois Rois
13006 Marseille France
Phone: 04 91 58 37 56

#371
Studio 37
Cuisines: French
Average price: Modest
Area: La Belle de Mai
Address: 37 rue Guibal
13001 Marseille France
Phone: 04 91 64 74 05

#372
Brasserie le Turf
Cuisines: Sushi Bar, Brasserie
Average price: Modest
Area: Sainte Anne
Address: 412 avenue Mazargues
13008 Marseille France
Phone: 04 91 77 93 26

#373
Azumi Sushi
Cuisines: Sushi Bar, Food Delivery Service,
Japanese, Fast Food
Average price: Modest
Area: Saint Barnabé
Address: 49 ave de St Barnabé
13012 Marseille France
Phone: 04 91 85 31 14

#374
Pizzéria du Marché
Cuisines: Pizza
Average price: Inexpensive
Area: Noailles
Address: 22 rue Feuillants
13001 Marseille France
Phone: 04 91 33 24 84

#375
Coco Loco
Cuisines: Burgers, Pizza, American
Average price: Inexpensive
Area: Saint Mauront
Address: 207 bd de Plombières
13003 Marseille France
Phone: 04 91 34 50 00

#376
Le Crystal
Cuisines: Cocktail Bar, French, American
Average price: Modest
Area: Hotel de Ville
Address: 148 Quai Port
13002 Marseille France
Phone: 04 91 91 57 96

#377
Habib's
Cuisines: Tea Room, Barbeque, Halal
Average price: Modest
Area: Saint Victor
Address: 26 quai de Rive Neuve
13007 Marseille France
Phone: 04 91 33 96 85

#378
Bar André
Cuisines: Sports Bar, Cafe
Average price: Modest
Area: Hotel de Ville, Les Grandes Carmes
Address: 25 Rue du Panier
13002 Marseille France
Phone: 04 91 90 34 38

#379
Le Troquet
Cuisines: Bar, French
Average price: Inexpensive
Area: Baille
Address: 17 place Pierre Roux
13005 Marseille France
Phone: 04 91 00 00 00

#380
Planetalis
Cuisines: Fast Food, Salad, Sandwiches
Average price: Inexpensive
Area: Belsunce
Address: 17 cours Belsunce
13001 Marseille France
Phone: 04 91 90 38 07

#381
La Cantine des Docks
Cuisines: French
Average price: Modest
Area: La Joliette
Address: 63 bd Robert Chuman
13002 Marseille France
Phone: 04 91 90 31 16

#382
Nah Trang Plage
Cuisines: Vietnamese
Average price: Modest
Area: Bonneveine
Address: 153 Ave Joseph Vidal
13008 Marseille France
Phone: 04 91 73 62 55

#383
Sard'In
Cuisines: Wine Bar, Cafe
Average price: Modest
Area: Hotel de Ville
Address: 32 rue de la Coutellerie
13002 Marseille France
Phone: 04 91 91 70 77

#384
Chez Paul
Cuisines: French
Average price: Modest
Area: Opéra
Address: 23 rue Saint-Saëns
13001 Marseille France
Phone: 04 88 08 36 65

#385
AM par Alexandre Mazzia
Cuisines: European, French
Average price: Exclusive
Area: Saint Giniez
Address: 9 rue François Rocca
13008 Marseille France
Phone: 04 91 24 83 63

#386
MetSens
Cuisines: Bistro
Average price: Modest
Area: Arenc
Address: 9 quai du Lazaret
13002 Marseille France
Phone: 04 91 45 76 48

#387
Dar Nejma
Cuisines: Moroccan
Average price: Expensive
Area: Notre Dame du Mont
Address: 15 Cours Julien
13006 Marseille France
Phone: 04 91 48 55 36

#388
Les Delices du Panier
Cuisines: Mediterranean
Average price: Modest
Area: Hotel de Ville, Les Grandes Carmes
Address: 27 rue du Panier
13002 Marseille France
Phone: 04 91 31 99 71

#389
L'Annexe
Cuisines: French
Average price: Modest
Area: Opéra
Address: 38A Place Thiars
13001 Marseille France
Phone: 04 91 55 52 10

#390
O'Pédalo
Cuisines: French, Mediterranean
Average price: Modest
Area: La Pointe Rouge
Address: 12 ave Montredon
13008 Marseille France
Phone: 04 91 73 19 44

#391
Allo Nem
Cuisines: Vietnamese
Average price: Modest
Area: La Conception
Address: 189 rue Saint Pierre
13005 Marseille France
Phone: 04 91 47 77 77

#392
Khai Hoan
Cuisines: Vietnamese
Average price: Modest
Area: Hotel de Ville
Address: 7 rue Bonneterie
13002 Marseille France
Phone: 04 91 91 01 32

#393
Le Bistrot Saint-Jacques
Cuisines: Bistro, French
Average price: Modest
Area: Préfecture
Address: 29 rue Saint-Jacques
13006 Marseille France
Phone: 04 91 37 08 72

#394
Sushi Shop
Cuisines: Sushi Bar, Japanese
Average price: Expensive
Area: Opéra
Address: 24 rue Lulli
13001 Marseille France
Phone: 08 26 82 66 28

#395
Le New Palace
Cuisines: Dance Club, Bar, Cafe
Average price: Modest
Area: Thier
Address: 10 Place Jean-Jaurès
13001 Marseille France
Phone: 04 96 12 46 34

#396
Blé d'Or
Cuisines: Italian, Pizza
Average price: Modest
Area: Bompard
Address: 2 place Saint Eugène
13007 Marseille France
Phone: 04 91 52 63 91

#397
Club House Vieux Port
Cuisines: French, Buffet
Average price: Modest
Area: Hotel de Ville
Address: 150 quai du Port
13002 Marseille France
Phone: 04 13 20 11 32

#398
Chez Claire
Cuisines: Seafood
Average price: Modest
Area: La Belle de Mai
Address: 12 rue d'Orange
13003 Marseille France
Phone: 06 12 53 34 10

#399
Le Comptoir des Docks
Cuisines: Tapas/Small Plates
Average price: Modest
Area: La Joliette
Address: 10 place de la Joliette
13002 Marseille France
Phone: 04 91 45 96 12

#400
BO&CO
Cuisines: French
Average price: Modest
Area: Arenc
Address: 232 bd de Paris
13002 Marseille France
Phone: 06 64 54 46 46

#401
A l'Angle
Cuisines: Pizza
Average price: Expensive
Area: Notre Dame du Mont
Address: 3 rue Crudère
13006 Marseille France
Phone: 07 82 48 18 25

#402
Le Fétiche
Cuisines: French, Seafood
Average price: Expensive
Area: Opéra
Address: 7 rue Paix Marcel Paul
13001 Marseille France
Phone: 04 91 54 00 98

#403
Hosteria
Cuisines: Italian, Mediterranean
Average price: Expensive
Area: Les Cinq Avenues
Address: 44 boulevard Philippon
13004 Marseille France
Phone: 04 91 64 66 28

#404
Le Pacifique 4
Cuisines: Asian Fusion, Buffet
Average price: Modest
Area: Pont de Vivaux
Address: 210 bd Romain Rolland
13010 Marseille France
Phone: 04 91 22 22 23

#405
Maracuja
Cuisines: Fast Food
Average price: Modest
Area: Castellane
Address: 185 Rue Paradis
13006 Marseille France
Phone: 09 84 12 13 14

#406
Le Peano
Cuisines: Pizza, Italian
Average price: Modest
Area: Opéra
Address: 16 rue Fortia
13001 Marseille France
Phone: 04 91 33 17 97

#407
Fuxia
Cuisines: Italian
Average price: Modest
Area: Opéra
Address: 27 rue Saint-Saëns
13001 Marseille France
Phone: 04 91 55 02 63

#408
Sousse Palace
Cuisines: Arabian, French
Average price: Modest
Area: Noailles
Address: 5 rue Papère
13001 Marseille France
Phone: 04 88 44 77 94

#409
Muy Heng
Cuisines: Chinese, Vietnamese
Average price: Modest
Area: La Joliette
Address: 51 avenue Robert Schuman
13002 Marseille France
Phone: 04 91 91 01 30

#410
Pizzeria les Deux Frangins
Cuisines: Food Delivery Service, Pizza
Average price: Modest
Area: Bompard
Address: 60 boulevard Bompard
13007 Marseille France
Phone: 04 91 52 66 98

#411
Le Chti Resto
Cuisines: French
Average price: Inexpensive
Area: Hotel de Ville
Address: 54 rue Caisserie
13002 Marseille France
Phone: 04 91 45 49 35

#412
L'Enoteka
Cuisines: Beer, Wine & Spirits,
Wine Bar, Bistro
Average price: Expensive
Area: Palais de Justice
Address: 28 bd Notre Dame
13006 Marseille France
Phone: 04 91 91 62 08

#413
Le Rhul
Cuisines: Seafood, Provencal
Average price: Expensive
Area: Le Roucas Blanc
Address: 269 Corniche Kennedy
13007 Marseille France
Phone: 04 91 52 54 54

#414
Adelizia
Cuisines: Italian, Delicatessen
Average price: Modest
Area: Le Pharo
Address: 12 rue César Aleman
13007 Marseille France
Phone: 06 16 54 04 64

#415
Le Pacifique
Cuisines: Chinese
Average price: Modest
Area: La Pomme
Address: 48 avenue Emmanuel Allard
13011 Marseille France
Phone: 04 91 35 03 38

#416
Ô Saveurs du Liban
Cuisines: Lebanese
Average price: Modest
Area: Opéra
Address: 1 rue Fortia
13001 Marseille France
Phone: 04 91 33 02 17

#417
La Tour de Jade
Cuisines: Chinese
Average price: Modest
Area: Hotel de Ville
Address: 236 Quai du Port
13002 Marseille France
Phone: 04 91 90 14 10

#418
Paella Montoya
Cuisines: Spanish, Food Truck
Average price: Modest
Area: Le Camas
Address: Place Jean Jaures
13006 Marseille France
Phone: 06 20 56 04 36

#419
Le Rhul
Cuisines: Hotels, Mediterranean
Average price: Expensive
Area: Endoume
Address: 269 Corniche John Kennedy
13007 Marseille France
Phone: 04 91 52 01 77

#420
Le Prince
Cuisines: Halal, Kebab, Pizza
Average price: Inexpensive
Area: Belsunce
Address: 36 Cours Belsunce
13001 Marseille France
Phone: 04 91 91 37 21

#421
Via Roma
Cuisines: Italian
Average price: Modest
Area: La Vieille Chapelle
Address: 19 Avenue de la Pointe Rouge
13008 Marseille France
Phone: 04 91 72 33 91

#422
Mezzo Di Pasta
Cuisines: Fast Food, Italian, Food Stand
Average price: Inexpensive
Area: Noailles
Address: 9 rue Pavillon
13001 Marseille France
Phone: 04 91 54 13 44

#423
Café Edmond
Cuisines: Cafe
Average price: Inexpensive
Area: Castellane
Address: 31 rue Dragon
13006 Marseille France
Phone: 04 91 37 74 95

#424
Le Pytheas
Cuisines: Brasserie, Cafe
Average price: Modest
Area: Opéra
Address: 2 rue Pytheas
13001 Marseille France
Phone: 04 91 54 15 70

#425
Le Moyen Orient
Cuisines: Lebanese
Average price: Modest
Area: Opéra
Address: 20 rue Paix Marcel Paul
13001 Marseille France
Phone: 04 91 33 28 87

#426
New Best Of
Cuisines: French, Desserts
Average price: Modest
Area: Castellane
Address: 7 place Castellane
13006 Marseille France
Phone: 04 91 42 46 89

#427
Chez Roger
Cuisines: Seafood, French
Average price: Expensive
Area: Hotel de Ville
Address: 28 quai Port
13002 Marseille France
Phone: 04 91 90 60 16

#428
Sri Ganesh
Cuisines: Indian, Food Delivery Service
Average price: Modest
Area: Opéra
Address: 25 place Huiles
13001 Marseille France
Phone: 04 91 33 09 15

#429
François Coquillages
Cuisines: Cafe
Average price: Expensive
Area: Castellane
Address: 25 Avenue Prado
13006 Marseille France
Phone: 04 91 79 22 57

#430
Lilin
Cuisines: Chinese, Wok
Average price: Modest
Area: Opéra
Address: 22 rue Sainte
13001 Marseille France
Phone: 04 91 56 59 66

#431
La Daurade
Cuisines: Seafood
Average price: Expensive
Area: Opéra
Address: 8 place Fortia
13001 Marseille France
Phone: 04 91 33 82 42

#432
Il Topolino
Cuisines: Cafe
Average price: Inexpensive
Area: Menpenti
Address: 59 Chemin Argile
13010 Marseille France
Phone: 04 91 75 93 97

#433
Marseille Nature
Les Amis de Georges
Cuisines: Vegetarian
Average price: Modest
Area: La Conception
Address: 19 place Gouffé
13005 Marseille France
Phone: 04 91 78 28 28

#434
Oki
Cuisines: Japanese
Average price: Modest
Area: La Joliette
Address: 59 ave Robert Schuman
13002 Marseille France
Phone: 04 91 90 29 10

#435
Caffé Noir
Cuisines: French
Average price: Modest
Area: Noailles
Address: 29 rue Palud
13001 Marseille France
Phone: 04 91 04 08 66

#436
La cuisine au beurre
Cuisines: Seafood, French
Average price: Expensive
Area: Hotel de Ville
Address: 72 Quai du Port
13002 Marseille France
Phone: 04 91 90 95 29

#437
Le Café Barok
Cuisines: Brasserie
Average price: Modest
Area: Castellane
Address: 6 avenue Jules Cantini
13006 Marseille France
Phone: 04 91 75 29 94

#438
Les Trottoirs Marseillais
Cuisines: Mediterranean
Average price: Expensive
Area: La Pointe Rouge
Address: 5 place Joseph Vidal
13008 Marseille France
Phone: 04 91 73 00 81

#439
Au Doyen
Cuisines: French
Average price: Modest
Area: Hotel de Ville
Address: 176 quai du Port
13002 Marseille France
Phone: 04 91 91 53 38

#440
Casanostra
Cuisines: French
Average price: Modest
Area: Le Rouet
Address: 195 rue Rouet
13008 Marseille France
Phone: 04 91 25 63 35

#441
Cthaï
Cuisines: Thai, Food Delivery Service
Average price: Modest
Area: Castellane, Lodi
Address: 1 rue de Gênes
13006 Marseille France
Phone: 04 91 26 77 59

#442
Yoj By Yoji
Cuisines: Japanese
Average price: Modest
Area: Arenc
Address: 9 quai du Lazaret
13002 Marseille France
Phone: 04 91 90 09 09

#443
Sushi Maki
Cuisines: Japanese
Average price: Modest
Area: Préfecture
Address: 4 rue Edmond Rostand
13006 Marseille France
Phone: 04 91 57 11 79

#444
Le Baobab
Cuisines: African
Average price: Inexpensive
Area: Les Réformés
Address: 3 Traverse St Bazile
13001 Marseille France
Phone: 04 91 50 44 76

#445
Chez Picone
Cuisines: Pizza, French, Italian
Average price: Modest
Area: Thier
Address: 120 la Canebière
13001 Marseille France
Phone: 04 91 48 77 05

#446
Le Patacrêpe - Castellane
Cuisines: Creperies, Sandwiches
Average price: Modest
Area: Castellane
Address: 19 place Castellane
13006 Marseille France
Phone: 04 91 79 59 93

#447
Le Joker
Cuisines: Burgers, American, Vegetarian
Average price: Modest
Area: Notre Dame du Mont
Address: 57 cours Julien
13006 Marseille France
Phone: 04 91 48 56 16

#448
Studio B Café
Cuisines: Cafe, Brasserie, Pizza
Average price: Modest
Area: Opéra
Address: 6 place du Général de Gaulle
13001 Marseille France
Phone: 04 91 33 06 50

#449
Le Cabanon du Cours
Cuisines: Mediterranean
Average price: Modest
Area: Notre Dame du Mont
Address: 13 bis rue Vian
13006 Marseille France
Phone: 04 91 02 25 21

#450
Le Jardin
Cuisines: French
Average price: Modest
Area: Mazargues
Address: 66 rue Sébastien Marcaggi
13009 Marseille France
Phone: 04 86 77 36 22

#451
Yamato
Cuisines: Japanese
Average price: Modest
Area: Notre Dame du Mont
Address: 3-5 place Notre Dame du Mont
13006 Marseille France
Phone: 04 91 42 34 84

#452
Spok Notre Dame
Cuisines: Fast Food
Average price: Modest
Area: Palais de Justice
Address: 67 bd Notre Dame
13006 Marseille France
Phone: 04 91 67 32 57

#453
Hippopotamus
Cuisines: Steakhouse
Average price: Expensive
Area: Opéra
Address: 7 Quai Belges
13001 Marseille France
Phone: 04 91 59 91 40

#454
L'Esquinade
Cuisines: Mediterranean, Seafood
Average price: Modest
Area: Opéra
Address: 38 place Thiars
13001 Marseille France
Phone: 04 91 33 28 82

#455
Le Bistronome
Cuisines: Bistro
Average price: Expensive
Area: Hotel de Ville
Address: 5 place Sadi Carnot
13002 Marseille France
Phone: 04 91 52 47 49

#456
Brasserie Le Soleil
Cuisines: Cafe
Average price: Modest
Area: Opéra
Address: 27 Quai Belges
13001 Marseille France
Phone: 04 91 55 06 92

#457
La Riviera
Cuisines: Cafe
Average price: Modest
Area: La Pointe Rouge
Address: place Joseph Vidal
13008 Marseille France
Phone: 04 91 73 27 27

#458
Le Petit Plat
Cuisines: Brasserie
Average price: Expensive
Area: Le Rouet
Address: 285 avenue Prado
13008 Marseille France
Phone: 04 91 79 44 71

#459
La Réserve
Cuisines: Cafe
Average price: Exclusive
Area: Le Roucas Blanc
Address: 200 Corniche Kennedy
13007 Marseille France
Phone: 04 91 16 19 21

#460
Brasserie de l'Alcazar
Cuisines: French, Cafe
Average price: Modest
Area: Belsunce
Address: 2 place François Mireur
13002 Marseille France
Phone: 04 91 91 80 88

#461
O' Ventre Sur Pâte
Cuisines: Pizza
Average price: Modest
Area: Bompard, Le Roucas Blanc
Address: 263 Chemin du Vallon de l'Oriol
13007 Marseille France
Phone: 09 80 47 13 72

#462
Place aux Huiles
Cuisines: Cafe, Grocery
Average price: Expensive
Area: Hotel de Ville
Address: 2 place Daviel
13001 Marseille France
Phone: 04 91 33 26 44

#463
Pizzéria Maga
Cuisines: Brasserie, Pizza
Average price: Modest
Area: Castellane
Address: 5 avenue Prado
13006 Marseille France
Phone: 04 91 80 37 00

#464
Le Bol d'or
Cuisines: Asian Fusion
Average price: Modest
Area: Lodi
Address: 50 cours Gouffé
13006 Marseille France
Phone: 04 91 78 86 90

#465
Kalipita
Cuisines: Greek
Average price: Modest
Area: Opéra
Address: 46 rue Vacon
13001 Marseille France
Phone: 09 50 46 90 11

#466
Albert Café
Cuisines: Mediterranean
Average price: Modest
Area: Endoume
Address: 6 rue des Flots Bleus
13007 Marseille France
Phone: 04 91 99 22 00

#467
Le Réservoir
Cuisines: Wine Bar, French
Average price: Modest
Area: Belsunce
Address: 22 rueThubaneau
13001 Marseille France
Phone: 04 91 90 71 18

#468
Café République
Cuisines: Mediterranean, Sports Bar, French
Average price: Modest
Area: La Joliette
Address: 123 rue de L'Évêché
13002 Marseille France
Phone: 04 91 90 52 70

#469
Spok
Cuisines: Soup, Juice Bar & Smoothies
Average price: Modest
Area: Opéra
Address: 7 rue Lulli
13001 Marseille France
Phone: 04 91 55 64 24

#470
La Serenata
Cuisines: French
Average price: Expensive
Area: La Vieille Chapelle
Address: 37 Pointe Rouge
13008 Marseille France
Phone: 04 91 75 79 05

#471
Bar du Marché
Cuisines: Bar, French
Average price: Inexpensive
Area: Notre Dame du Mont
Address: 15 place Notre Dame du Mont
13006 Marseille France
Phone: 04 91 92 58 89

#472
Corner Baille
Cuisines: Burgers, Bistro
Average price: Modest
Area: Baille
Address: 262 bd Baille
13005 Marseille France
Phone: 04 91 79 61 24

#473
Le Vientiane
Cuisines: Vietnamese, Thai, Laotian
Average price: Modest
Area: Hotel de Ville
Address: 14 rue de la Mure
13002 Marseille France
Phone: 04 91 90 89 13

#474
Restaurant Lou Granjoun
Cuisines: French
Average price: Inexpensive
Area: Le Camas
Address: 62 rue George
13005 Marseille France
Phone: 04 91 42 48 74

#475
Zia Concetta
Cuisines: Trattorie, Imported Food
Average price: Modest
Area: Bompard
Address: 315 corniche Kennedy
13007 Marseille France
Phone: 04 91 19 84 45

#476
Le Charles Livon
Cuisines: French
Average price: Expensive
Area: Le Pharo
Address: 89 bd Charles Livon
13007 Marseille France
Phone: 04 91 52 22 41

#477
Le Marseillais
Cuisines: French
Average price: Expensive
Area: Opéra
Address: 2 quai de Rive Neuve
13001 Marseille France
Phone: 04 91 90 72 99

#478
Le Champoreau
Cuisines: Brasserie
Average price: Inexpensive
Area: La Joliette
Address: 11 place de la Joliette
13002 Marseille France
Phone: 04 91 90 25 01

#479
Au Royaume de la Chantilly
Cuisines: Cheese Shop, French
Average price: Expensive
Area: La Panouse
Address: 11 bd du Redon
13009 Marseille France
Phone: 04 91 25 66 61

#480
Living Art's
Cuisines: Jazz & Blues, French, Wine Bar
Average price: Expensive
Area: Notre Dame du Mont
Address: 50 cours Julien
13006 Marseille France
Phone: 09 52 82 35 49

#481
La Maison
Cuisines: European, Mediterranean
Average price: Expensive
Area: La Plage
Address: 21 promenade Georges Pompidou
13008 Marseille France
Phone: 04 91 22 52 03

#482
Brasserie du Village
Cuisines: Brasserie
Average price: Modest
Area: Saint Barnabé
Address: 7 rue Léon Meisserel
13012 Marseille France
Phone: 04 91 34 40 40

#483
En Nour
Cuisines: Mediterranean, Caterer,
Middle Eastern
Average price: Inexpensive
Area: Noailles
Address: 11 rue de l'Académie
13001 Marseille France
Phone: 06 29 31 77 90

#484
Ô Zen la République
Cuisines: Buffet, Asian Fusion, Sushi Bar
Average price: Modest
Area: Hotel de Ville
Address: 1 place Sadi Carnot
13002 Marseille France
Phone: 04 91 45 40 96

#485
Dubble
Cuisines: Fast Food
Average price: Modest
Area: La Plage
Address: 515 avenue Prado
13008 Marseille France
Phone: 04 91 77 98 76

#486
Regard Café
Cuisines: Bistro
Average price: Expensive
Area: La Joliette
Address: Musée Regards de Provence
13002 Marseille France
Phone: 04 96 17 40 45

#487
Subway
Cuisines: Fast Food
Average price: Modest
Area: Castellane
Address: 187 rue Rome
13006 Marseille France
Phone: 04 96 12 02 86

#488
Bikini café
Cuisines: Bar, Bistro, Tobacco Shop
Average price: Modest
Area: Opéra
Address: 1 Rue Breteuil
13001 Marseille France
Phone: 04 91 33 84 98

#489
Le Logis du Panier
Cuisines: French, Cajun/Creole
Average price: Modest
Area: Les Grandes Carmes
Address: 19 rue Puits-du-Denier
13002 Marseille France
Phone: 06 21 07 08 87

#490
La Butte Rouge
Cuisines: Tapas/Small Plates
Average price: Exclusive
Area: Thier
Address: 11 rue des Trois Mages
13001 Marseille France
Phone: 04 91 47 29 66

#491
Spok
Cuisines: Sandwiches
Average price: Inexpensive
Area: Baille
Address: 1 rue Crillon
13005 Marseille France
Phone: 04 91 98 20 87

#492
L'Entrecôte
Cuisines: Steakhouse, French
Average price: Modest
Area: Opéra
Address: 9 quai Belges
13001 Marseille France
Phone: 04 91 33 31 33

#493
Via Mermoz
Cuisines: Italian
Average price: Expensive
Area: Périer
Address: 4 rue Jean Mermoz
13008 Marseille France
Phone: 04 91 37 88 33

#494
O'Cours Ju
Cuisines: Bar, Cafe, Coffee & Tea
Average price: Inexpensive
Area: Notre Dame du Mont
Address: 67 Cours Julien
13006 Marseille France
Phone: 04 91 48 48 58

#495
Chez Angèle
Cuisines: Mediterranean, Pizza, Italian
Average price: Modest
Area: Hotel de Ville
Address: 50 rue Caisserie
13002 Marseille France
Phone: 04 91 90 63 35

#496
Pizza Zazza
Cuisines: Pizza, Food Delivery Service
Average price: Modest
Area: Baille
Address: 244 boulevard Baille
13005 Marseille France
Phone: 04 91 78 35 35

#497
E-Wine
Cuisines: Tapas Bar
Average price: Modest
Area: Notre Dame du Mont
Address: 94 cours Julien
13006 Marseille France
Phone: 04 96 12 08 47

#498
Le 26 Café
Cuisines: Bistro, French
Average price: Modest
Area: Saint Victor
Address: 26 avenue de la corse
13007 Marseille France
Phone: 04 86 12 35 30

#499
Eating
Cuisines: Fast Food
Average price: Modest
Area: Palais de Justice
Address: 40 rue Montgrand
13006 Marseille France
Phone: 04 91 33 76 88

#500
Mido
Cuisines: Fast Food, Mediterranean, Halal
Average price: Inexpensive
Area: Notre Dame du Mont
Address: 70 cours Julien
13006 Marseille France
Phone: 04 91 42 45 89

Printed in Great Britain
by Amazon